Learn About

BUTTERFLIES
IN THE
GARDEN

Brenda Dziedzic

Author: Brenda Dziedzic
Printer: Sheridan Books, Inc.

Published by: Brenda Dziedzic in Westland, MI 48186

Library of Congress Control Number: 2011902775

Dziedzic, Brenda
    Learn About Butterflies In The Garden / Brenda Dziedzic.

ISBN 978-0-615-44303-4

Book Design by Brenda Dziedzic

Maps and Illustrations by Brenda Dziedzic

Printed in the United States of America

I dedicate this book to

Lois Hansen

who got me started

in this wonderful world

of

Butterflies

To Karen + Joan,

Happy Butterflying,

Brenda Dziedzic

Contents

Preface

I always had a love for nature and in the late summer of 2001 the thought came to me that I would like to see lots of butterflies like I used to see as a child. What could I do? I decided to create a butterfly garden and went out and I bought my first three butterfly bushes. That winter I did a lot of research on the internet to find out what other kinds of plants I would need. In the early spring of 2002, I took my list of plants to a gardening store to buy seeds to start, that I thought were necessary for a butterfly garden. I met Lois Hansen there and she started me in the right direction of learning about butterflies. She told me that most of the plants on my list would not attract butterflies. She then gave me a list of necessary plants for my garden. I had no idea where to purchase these plants from, so Lois gave me several names of native plant nurseries, and also said she would give me some of her plants. A few months later she brought over some plants from her garden, and my very first two Monarch eggs. She also brought over several books for me to read, which were about butterflies. That was it. I was hooked. From then on I began reading every book I could find about butterflies.

Each year, I increase my variety of host and nectar plants. I bring into my home most of the eggs that I find, so that I can help the butterflies, since a lot of their habitat is being destroyed. I have learned a lot of information about butterflies by observing their life cycles. Even though I have a small city lot, which is 60 ft. x 120 ft., I have a variety of butterflies in my yard because of the diversity of host plants. If they can complete their life cycle in your yard, you'll have more than you would by only having nectar plants. Anyone can also have a variety of butterflies in their yard by planting the plants that butterflies use. From 2002 through 2010, I raised 2909 butterflies. When they come out of their chrysalis, I release them back to the garden.

I am a co-founder and president of SEMBA (Southeast Michigan Butterfly Association), a member of NABA (North American Butterfly Association), MES (Michigan Entomological Society), The Lepidopterists' Society, WAM (Wildflower Association of Michigan), Wild Ones, and I'm an Advanced Master Gardener. My yard is certified by Monarch Watch as a Monarch Waystation, SEMBA as a Native Butterfly Garden and as a Wildlife Habitat by the National Wildlife Federation.

I have given talks at Master Gardener meetings, nurseries, garden clubs, city leisure services, DTE Energy company, and schools on butterfly gardening. I have also built a website, http://ButterfliesInThe-Garden.com, which has butterfly related information on. I try to share my knowledge about butterfly plants and rearing butterflies with as many people as I can. We need to give back to the earth. We can do this by planting the native plants that were intended to be here. Native plants have a higher nectar content than most non-natives and they produce a healthy ecosystem by attracting a wider variety of birds and insects, which enhance the biodiversity.

Acknowledgements

I would like to thank my father and mother (John Sattler and Margaret Sattler) for teaching me to respect and love all that God has created. It is this love that has enabled me to devote my life to studying butterflies. I want to thank them also, in part, for making it possible for me to publish this book.

I also want to thank my husband (James Dziedzic) for his support as I spent endless hours in my butterfly garden, raising butterflies, studying butterflies, and Butterflying in the field.

Photographs are by Brenda Dziedzic, except where noted.

Photographer and page number:

Angela Gross: 30 (Tiger Swallowtail - bottom), 262 (Cecropia Moths), 263 (Cecropia Moth - top & bottom), **Berry Nall**: 45 (Pipevine Swallowtail eggs - top & bottom), 158 (Julia Heliconian caterpillar), 188 (Pearl Crescent caterpillar), 194 (Queen chrysalis), **Burris & Richards** (www.ButterflyNature.com): 117 (Baltimore Checkerspot eggs & caterpillars - all), 119 (Baltimore Checkerspot chrysalis), 145 (Great Spangled Fritillary eggs - top & bottom left), **Carol Clements**: 146 (Great Spangled Fritillary caterpillar - bottom), **D. H. Janzen:** 75 (Great Southern White caterpillars), **David M. Wright**: 103 (Summer Azure egg), 104 (Summer Azure pupae), **Dunia Garcia**: 76 (Great Southern White caterpillar - top), **Glenn M. Richardson**: 138 (Eastern Comma eggs - both), 139 (Eastern Comma caterpillar - both), 146 (Great Spangled Fritillary caterpillar - top), **Jan Dauphin**: 55 (Polydamas Swallowtail chrysalis), **Jaret C. Daniels, Ph.D.**: 76 (Great Southern White caterpillar - bottom), 235 (Zebra Heliconian caterpillar - bottom), **Marcie O'Connor** (www.aprairiehaven.com): 175 (Mourning Cloak chrysalis), **NC Division of Parks and Recreation** photo by: **Ed Corey**: 133 (Common Wood Nymph caterpillar), **Peter Bryant**: 173 (Mourning Cloak eggs - both), 174 (Mourning Cloak caterpillars - top), **Ron Hemberger**: 174 (Mourning Cloak caterpillar © 2008 - bottom), **Rose Maschek**: 187 (Pearl Crescent - laying eggs), 188 (Pearl Crescent eggs), **William Flores**: 53 (Polydamas Swallowtail eggs - top), 54 (Polydamas Swallowtail caterpillars - top left & right).

Introduction

Butterflies and moths make up the insect order Lepidoptera. Lepidoptera is derived from the Greek words "lepido" for scale and "ptera" for wings.

The Differences between Butterflies and Moths

These are the major differences between butterflies and moths, but there are exceptions.

Generally butterflies are diurnal (day flying), have thin smooth bodies, hold their wings upright over their back when at rest, are colorful, and have clubbed antennae. Moths most generally are nocturnal (night flying), have fat hairy bodies, fold the wings tent-like over their back or wrap them over their body, are dull colored, and have threadlike or feathery antennae.

Butterfly Life Cycle

Butterflies undergo a complete metamorphosis. This consists of four distinct stages. These stages are egg (ovum), caterpillar (larva), chrysalis (pupa), and adult (imago).

Egg

The eggs are various shapes, colors, and sizes. Some of shapes and textures are: barrel, conical, elongated, oval with a flat bottom, spherical, sculptured, and smooth. There are many colors. Some of the colors are: beige, cream, green, light green, light yellow, turquoise, and white. The sizes range from about 1/64 inch to a little over 1/16 inch.

Caterpillar

A caterpillar has three parts. These parts are the head, thorax, and abdomen. The head has six pair of simple eyes (ocelli). Even though they have six pair of eyes, their vision

is poor. It also has a spinneret that produces silk. The body consists of thirteen segments. There are three thoracic segments and ten abdominal segments. The thorax has three pair of true legs, and the abdomen has five pair of prolegs. The prolegs have very small hooks that enable the caterpillar to hold onto a leaf or a silk mat. Spiracles are holes in the sides of the thorax and abdomen that the caterpillars receive oxygen through.

Caterpillars usually go through five instars. Instars are periods of growth between molting. They have exoskeletons, so when they become too large for their skin, they molt. Molting is the act of shedding their skin. Before they molt, they attach to an object with silk. This helps them to crawl out of their old skin. After attaching to an object, they quit eating and do not move for usually at least one day. After that, they molt. When the caterpillar molts for the last time, it reveals its chrysalis.

Prechrysalis

Before molting for the last time, the caterpillar will seek out a safe place to make its chrysalis. They spin a silk button to attach the rear most pair of prolegs to. Some then hang downward in a J shape. Others will also spin a U shaped girdle, which they position between the first and second abdominal segments. This holds them upright.

Chrysalis

During their final molting, the skin splits and the chrysalis is revealed. The tissues break down and rearrange within the chrysalis and the butterfly is formed.

Adult

When the butterfly emerges from the chrysalis, the wings are very small and the body is large. As it pumps blood into the wings, the wings elongate and the body becomes smaller. After a few hours, the wings harden and become dry. It is then ready for flight.

Butterflies have a hard exoskeleton and three main body parts. The three main parts are the head, thorax, and abdomen. The head has two large compound eyes, a proboscis, and two clubbed antennae. A flexible straw-like structure, the proboscis, is used for drinking nectar and fluids. They use the antennae for smell, touch, and balance. Butterflies also smell with sense receptors which are located in their legs, and other parts of their body.

There are two pair of scaled wings and three pair of jointed legs on the thorax. The abdomen contains the reproductive, digestive, and excretory systems. Spiracles are breathing holes, which run along the side of the abdomen. At the end of the abdomen, the genitalia are located. The two structures of the male's genitalia are called claspers. The female has a notch.

Male

Female

Mating

Time Period of Each Stage

The life cycle of the butterflies and moths are dependent on temperatures. In this book the period of time for each stage is an average. In a cold environment each stage may take considerably longer.

Maps

On the maps, green indicates the region of each butterfly and moth.

Parts of the Butterfly

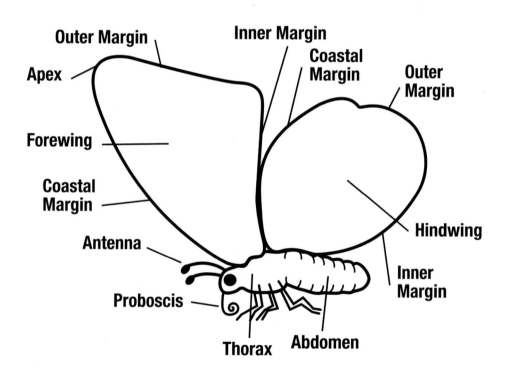

Areas of the Butterfly Wings

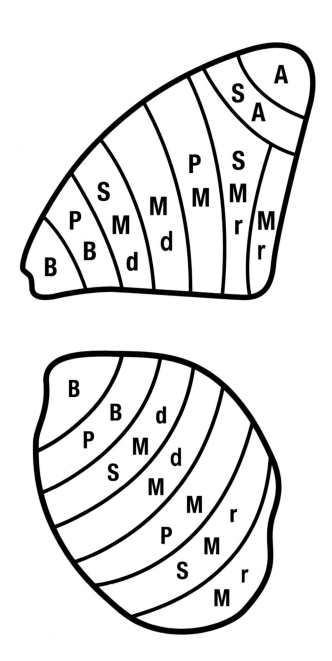

B - basal, PB - postbasal, SMd - submedian, Md - median, PM - postmedian, SMr - submarginal, Mr - marginal, SA - subapical, A - apical

Butterfly and Moth Families

Swallowtails

They are medium to large butterflies and most have hindwing tails. As they feed, most flutter their wings. All species visit flowers and males can be found puddling. With most of the species, the males patrol when looking for females. Some others, instead, perch on hilltops.

Eggs are usually spherical and smooth.

Young caterpillars mimic bird droppings, with their black bodies and white dorsal saddle. The caterpillars have an osmeterium. An osmeterium is an orangish forked gland behind the head, which emits a foul scent to repel predators.

Most of the time, the chrysalises are held upright with a silk girdle. The last brood of the year usually overwinters in the chrysalis stage.

Whites/Sulphurs

They are medium to small butterflies. All adult species nectar on flowers and the males often puddle. Males patrol when looking for females.

The eggs are generally elongated.

The caterpillars are usually greenish and covered with very short fine hair.

A silken girdle holds the chrysalis upright.

Blues

They are very small butterflies. While perched, they rub their hindwings together.

The caterpillars are usually slug-like and produce honeydew which the ants eat. In return, the ants protect them from predators and parasites.

Brushfoots

They are small to large butterflies. This family has more species than any other. All of this family has reduced forelegs that are covered with short hairs. They look like a bottle brush, hence the name, brushfoots.

Most of the time, the chrysalis of this family hangs downward from a silk pad.

Males are quite often territorial and aggressive.

Skippers

They are small to medium butterflies. The ends of the clubbed antennae are usually hooked. They have large eyes and stout bodies.

Males look for females by either perching or patrolling.

Adults have an erratic and quick flight.

Giant Silkworm Moths

They are medium to very large moths. Their body is densely covered with hair. Due to the reduced or absent proboscis, they do not feed. Many rest with their wings folded vertically over their body, while others horizontally spread both pair of wings.

Some pupate in silken cocoons, while others pupate in the soil.

Sphinx Moths

They are small to very large moths. Their wings are usually elongated and narrow. Most have large eyes, which aid in feeding. Some have a very long proboscis. This helps in pollination. Most are very strong fliers and can hover at flowers.

The eggs are usually round, smooth, and some shade of green.

They usually pupate in the soil, but some will form cocoons in leaf litter.

Tussock Moths

They are medium moths, with the female usually being larger than the male. Their proboscis is reduced or absent. They often incorporate their larval hairs in their cocoon.

Butterfly Gardening

To attract butterflies to your yard, it is important to plant nectar and host plants. Nectar plants provide food for the adults that pass through. Make sure you have plants that will blossom in each season, thus providing a continuous food supply. If you really want them to stay around, then you must plant host plants. These are the plants that they lay their eggs on and that the caterpillars feed on. Whenever possible, use native plants. Native plants can be economically a better choice because they don't require watering, fertilizer, or pesticides. They also attract beneficial insects which reduce pests and pollinate the plants. Some of the non-native plants have been genetically altered so that the nectar content may be minimal, if at all. For each butterfly listed in this book, I have included the Latin name of each host plant. That way you will be able to select the plants that are native to your area. Some other things you may want to incorporate in your butterfly garden are:

Lots of Sun - Most butterfly plants need at least 6 hours of sun each day.

Plant Arrangements - To easily observe the butterflies in your garden, plant the taller plants in the back.

Plant in Groups - It is easier for butterflies to see the plants when planted in groups of three or more, since butterflies are nearsighted.

Shelter from the Wind - Butterflies are delicate little creatures, so a little protection from the wind can help. For a wind barrier use trees, shrubs, tall plants, trellises, or fences.

Sunning Spot - Rocks and stepping stones can be used by butterflies to warm themselves, so they can fly when it is cool outside.

Place to Puddle - This can be a container holding sand, mulch, etc. that stays moist. Butterflies ingest minerals from damp sand, soil, mulch, and the like, which aides in reproduction.

Overripe Fruit - Setting out a container of overripe fruit, such as bananas, cantaloupe, peaches, pears, and watermelons, provides nutrients for butterflies.

The most important thing to remember is that butterflies and caterpillars are insects, so **NO PESTICIDES.**

Winter Preparation for Butterfly Gardens

I live in Westland Michigan and what I do with my garden, which is my whole yard except for paths, to get ready for winter is nothing. Different species of butterflies and moths overwinter differently. Some overwinter as an egg, some as a larva, some in a chrysalis, naked pupa, or a pupa within a cocoon, and some as adults. These wonderful little forms of Lepidoptera could be anywhere in the garden. They could be on plants, in leaf litter, or in the ground. I wait to break down my plants, which I drop to the ground to use as mulch, until sometime in April.

I have many trees, which I grow in pots. Because of the size of my yard, which is only 60 by 120 feet, I don't have room to plant these trees in the ground. I grow them because I want to have as many host plants as possible. That way I will have a large variety of butterflies.

Over 30 different species of butterflies visit my yard. The trees that I have in pots and the butterflies that lay their eggs on them are:

Choke Cherry (*Prunus virginiana*) and Wild Black Cherry (*Prunus serotina*) – Coral Hairstreak (*Satyrium titus*), Eastern Tiger Swallowtail (*Papilio glaucus*), Red-spotted Purple (*Limenitis arthemis*), and Striped Hairstreak (*Satyrium liparops*).

Sassafras (*Sassafras albidum*) – Spicebush Swallowtail (*Papilio troilus*).

Hop Tree (*Ptelea trifoliata*) and Prickly Ash (*Zanthoxylum americanum*) – Giant Swallowtail (*Papilio cresphontes*).

Chinquapin Oak (*Quercus muehlenbergii*) – Banded Hairstreak (*Satyrium calanus*), Edwards' Hairstreak (*Satyrium edwardsii*), and Juvenal's Dusky-wing (*Erynnis juvenalis*).

Tulip Tree (*Liriodendron tulipifera*) – Eastern Tiger Swallowtail (*Papilio glaucus*).

Hackberry (*Celtis occidentalis*) – American Snout (*Libytheana carinenta*), Hackberry Emperor (*Asterocampa celtis*), Mourning Cloak (*Nymphalis antiopa*), Question Mark (*Polygonia interrogationis*), and Tawny Emperor (*Asterocampa clyton*).

Black Willow (*Salix nigra*), Corkscrew Willow (*Salix matsudana*), Pussy Willow (*Salix discolor*), Sandbar Willow (*Salix interior*) – Dreamy Duskywing (*Erynnis icelus*), Mourning Cloak (*Nymphalis antiopa*), Red-spotted Purple (*Limenitis arthemis*), and Viceroy (*Limenitis archippus*).

To prepare for winter I move my potted trees, with a dolly, behind my garage. I place them right next to each other and put mulch in between the pots, around the pots, and over the pots. Putting the plants behind the garage and covering them with mulch helps to protect them from the wind and also keeps the roots warmer. The next spring when the leaves start growing, I move them back to the garden. Whenever my trees start looking distressed, I remove them from the pots, cut off about 1/3 of the roots, and repot them.

Raising Butterflies

If you see a butterfly touching a host plant, that's a good sign that it may be laying eggs. The female will generally curl the anal end of the abdomen as she deposits an egg.

If that is the case, break off a small piece of the leaf that has the egg on it and put it in a container. The container should be at least five inches tall, so that it provides enough room for the wings to expand when it emerges from the chrysalis. Turn the container on its side with the lid in the front and put a damp, not wet, paper towel on the bottom. Placing the leaf on the damp paper towel will keep it from drying out. You can also put some floral foam (for fresh flowers) in a small container. Fill it with water and then add some stems from the host plant to it and place it in the container. For some species, such as swallowtails, you may also want to put a twig diagonally in the container. Quite often, swallowtails will attach to branches to pupate.

Do not put any holes in the cage until the caterpillar is about a half inch long. When the caterpillars first hatch, they are so small; they can crawl out of a hole made with a sewing needle. Just open the container a couple times a day and wave the lid over it to circulate the air. When they reach a half inch or so, switch the lid with no holes to one with holes. I cut a hole in the lid and hot glue a piece of window screen to it. I have found that making the hole only about 2 x 2 inches provides enough moisture to keep the leaf fresh. It also insures that the top is dry enough so that the silk pad, which the chrysalis attaches to, is secure. As the caterpil-

lar eats, add more leaves as needed. Replace the paper towel when it becomes soiled. Dirty and wet conditions are unhealthy for caterpillars.

When the caterpillar is ready to make its chrysalis it will spin a silk pad to attach the anal prolegs to. Many species will hang downward in a J shape from the silk pad. Swallowtails will also spin a silk girdle, which holds them in an upright position. With many of the species, the night before they are going to emerge, the chrysalis will become transparent and you'll be able to see the wings. After it emerges, it will take a few hours for the wings to harden and dry. You can then release it back to your garden. If it is dark or raining, just wait until the next day. They'll be fine without food until then. If it should continue to rain for a couple of days, you can give them fruit punch Gatorade on a cotton ball. Just make sure you that you change the cotton ball every other day, so that bacteria don't build up on it. Before using your container to put another egg or caterpillar in, make sure that you soak it for at least 4 hours in a 20% bleach solution. Then rinse thoroughly. This will kill any bacteria or parasites that may be in the container. That's about all there is to it. Have fun and Happy Butterflying!

Black Swallowtail

Family - Swallowtails - *Papilionidae* (pap-ill-ee-ON-ah-dee)

Flight period: April - October

Black Swallowtail

Black Swallowtail
Papilio polyxenes (pa-pil-ee-oh • pol-ix-ee-nees)

The wingspan is 2 1/2 - 4 1/4 inches.

The dorsal/upperside is black, has orange hindwing eyespots with a black dot in the middle, a yellow spot near the tip of the forewing, and a black body with yellow spots. The male has two rows of yellow spots and a small amount of iridescent blue between the two rows on the hindwing. The female's two rows may be yellow or cream. The submarginal row is reduced and the iridescent blue on the hindwing is increased.

The ventral/underside is black. The forewing has cream spots The hindwing has cream spots on the marginal edge and two rows of orange spots with iridescent blue between them.

Host/Larval Food Plants

Carrot - *Daucus carota* var. *sativa*
Celery - *Apium graveolens* spp.
Common Rue - *Ruta graveolens*
Dill - *Anethum graveolens*
Fennel - *Foeniculum vulgare* spp.
Mock Bishop Weed - *Ptilimnium capillaceum*
Parsley - *Petroselinum crispum* spp.
Queen Anne's Lace - *Daucus carota*
Water Cowbane - *Oxypolis filiformis*
Wild Parsnip - *Pastinaca sativa*

Common Rue – *Ruta graveolens*

They have 2 broods each year. The egg is pale yellow and laid singly.

The egg is between 1/32 and 3/64 inch and takes 4 - 8 days to hatch.

When it hatches, the caterpillar is about 1/8 inch.

Earlier instars have a cream saddle and branched spines.

After molting, you can see the skin it just crawled out of and the pale yellow head capsule. Shortly, it will darken in color. As the caterpillar goes through each instar, its appearance will change.

The caterpillar stage is for 14 - 24 days. In the last instar, the caterpillar is about 2 inches.

The caterpillar attaches its rear end to a silk pad. It then spins silk threads to form a silk girdle, which holds it upright, in the prechrysalis stage.

It is revealing its chrysalis, as it molts for the last time.

The chrysalis can be shades of green or brown, even though they eat the same food and make their chrysalis on the same substrate.

The chrysalis stage can be as short as 10 days. If it is the last brood, which overwinters, it will not emerge until spring. There may also be times that the butterfly will not emerge until the following spring.

The chrysalis will become transparent before emerging.

Adult Food

They can be found puddling and also feed on Aster, Azalea, Blazing Star, Blue Mistflower, Brazilian Verbena, Butterfly Bush, Chives, Clover, Garden Phlox, Hyssop, Indian Blanket, Lantana, Milkweed, Monarda, Pentas, Porterweed, Purple Coneflower, Spirea, Sweet William, Thistle, and Zinnia.

Blue Mistflower – *Conoclinium coelestinum*

New England Aster – *Symphyotrichum novae-angliae*

Eastern Tiger Swallowtail

Family - Swallowtails - *Papilionidae* (pap-ill-ee-ON-ah-dee)

Flight period: April - October, deep south February - November

Eastern Tiger Swallowtail

Eastern Tiger Swallowtail
Papilio glaucus (pa-pil-ee-oh • glaw-kus)

The wingspan is 3 1/4 - 5 1/2 inches.

The dorsal/upperside, of all males and some females, is yellow with black tiger stripes. The hingwing has iridescent blue scaling, which is increased on the female. There is also a black form of the female, which is more common southward. The black form has a shadow of tiger stripes.

The ventral/underside of the forewing is similar to the dorsal. It has a row of marginal pale yellow spots and black wing margins. The hindwing has orange marginal spots and iridescent blue scaling.

Host/Larval Food Plants

Ash - *Fraxinus* spp.
Cherry - *Prunus* spp.
Cottonwood - *Populus* spp.
Hop Tree - *Ptelea trifoliata*
Lilac - *Syringa* spp.
Sweet Bay - *Magnolia virginiana*
Tulip Tree - *Liriodendron tulipifera*
Willow - *Salix* spp.

Egg on Common Lilac – *Syringa vulgaris*

They have 2 - 3 broods each year. The egg is light green, between 1/32 and 3/64 inch, and laid singly on the host leaf. It takes 5 - 10 days to hatch.

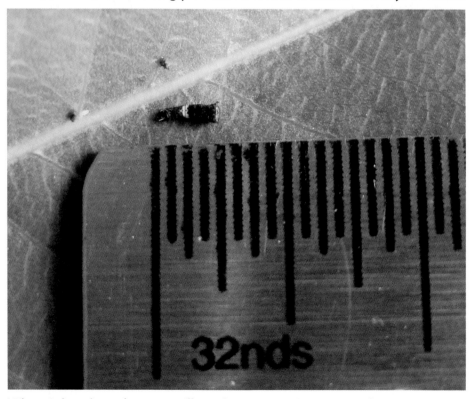

When it hatches, the caterpillar is between 3/32 - 1/8 inch.

The first thing the caterpillar does after hatching is eat its eggshell.

The caterpillar uses silk it produces to curl a leaf. It stays in that leaf when not eating. Earlier instars resemble bird droppings.

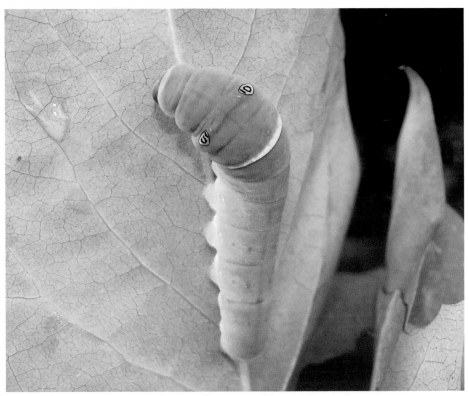

Later instars are snakelike. In the last instar, the caterpillar is about 2 inches. The caterpillar stage can be up to 46 days.

Right before the prechrysalis stage, the caterpillar turns grayish brown.

The chrysalis stage can be as short as 10 days. If it is the last brood, which overwinters, it will not emerge until spring.

Joe-Pye Weed - *Eupatorium maculatum*

Adult Food

They can be found puddling and also feed on Azalea, Blazing Star, Brazilian Verbena, Butterfly Bush, Buttonbush, Chives, Golden Dewdrop, Glossy Abelia, Honeysuckle, Ironweed, Joe-Pye Weed, Lantana, Lilac, Mexican Sunflower, Milkweed, New England Aster, Pentas, Porterweed, Prairie Phlox, Purple Coneflower, Spider Flower, Thistle, and Zinnia.

Butterfly Bush - *Buddleia davidii*

Giant Swallowtail

Family - Swallowtails - *Papilionidae* (pap-ill-ee-ON-ah-dee)

Flight period: April - October, all year deep south

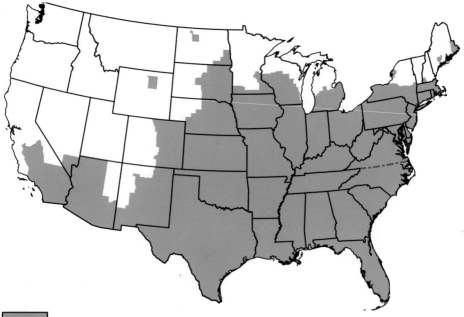

Giant Swallowtail

Giant Swallowtail
Papilio cresphontes (pa-pil-ee-oh • cres-fon-tees)

The wingspan is 4 - 6 1/4 inches.

The dorsal/upperside is blackish brown. It has a pale yellow ban across the forewings and a pale yellow diagonal band that starts at the tip of the forewing and ends at the anal edge of the hindwing. Near the anal edge of the hindwing, there is a reddish orange spot with blue above it and a black dot below it. The tails have a pale yellow spot. The female has more blue above the reddish orange spot than the male has.

The ventral/underside is pale yellow with blackish brown markings and a blue median hindwing band with orange markings on either side.

Host/Larval Food Plants

Citrus - *Citrus* spp.
Common Rue - *Ruta graveolens*
Hercules Club - *Zanthoxylum clava-herculis*
Hop Tree - *Ptelea trifoliata*
Lime Prickly-Ash - *Zanthoxylum fagara*
Prickly Ash - *Zanthoxylum americanum*
Torchwood - *Amyris elemifera*

Common Rue – *Ruta graveolens*

They have 2 - 3 broods each year. The egg is light yellowish tan to orangish brown and laid singly.

The egg is between 1/32 and 3/64 inch. It takes 4 - 9 days to hatch.

When it hatches, the caterpillar is about 1/8 inch.

After hatching the caterpillar will eat its eggshell.

The caterpillar looks like bird droppings which helps deter predators.

The caterpillar stage is for 18 - 26 days. In the last instar, the caterpillar is about 2 3/16 inches.

The caterpillar attaches its rear end to a silk pad. It then spins silk threads to form a silk girdle, which holds it upright in the prechrysalis stage.

The chrysalis stage can be as short as 14 days. If it is the last brood, which overwinters, it will not emerge until spring. There may also be times that the butterfly will not emerge until the following spring.

Within 15 minutes after it starts to eclose from the chrysalis the wings are completely expanded. It takes a few hours for the wings to harden and dry.

Adult Food

They can be found puddling and also feed on dung, rotting fruit, Azalea, Brazilian Verbena, Butterfly Bush, Buttonbush, Bougainvilla, Carolina Jasmine, Chives, Citrus, Firespike, Golden Dewdrop, Goldenrod, Joe-Pye Weed, Lantana, Mexican Sunflower, Milkweed, Monarda, Pentas, Porterweed, Purple Coneflower, Scabiosa, Thistle, and Zinnia.

Swamp Milkweed - *Asclepias incarnata*

Purple Coneflower – *Echinacea purpurea*

Profusion Apricot – *Zinnia angustifolia x elegans*

Pipevine Swallowtail

Family - Swallowtails - *Papilionidae* (pap-ill-ee-ON-ah-dee)

Flight period: April - October, deep south February - November

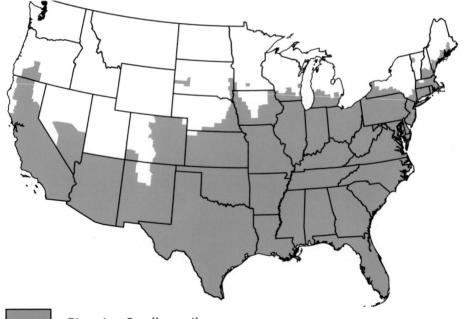

Pipevine Swallowtail

Pipevine Swallowtail
Battus philenor (bat-tus • fil-en-or)

The wingspan is 2 3/4 - 4 1/2 inches.

The dorsal/upperside is black with white marginal spots on the outer margins of both wings. The hindwing of the male is iridescent blue or greenish blue with submarginal white spots. The female is duller and has more prominent white submarginal spots.

The ventral/underside is black. The forewing is similar to the dorsal. The hindwing has greenish blue iridescent scales, a row of submarginal orange spots, and white marginal spots on the outer margin.

Host/Larval Food Plants

Dutchman's Pipe - *Aristolochia macrophylla*
Swanflower - *Aristolochia erecta*
Virginia Snakeroot - *Aristolochia serpentaria*
Watson's Dutchman's Pipe - *Aristolochia watsonii*
Wild Ginger - *Asarum canadense*
Wooly Pipevine - *Aristolochia tomentosa*
also other Pipevine - *Aristolochia* spp.

Pipevine – *Aristolochia* spp.

They have 2 broods each year in the north and 3 - 4 in the deep south. The eggs are brownish orange and laid singly or in clusters. They lay the eggs on the tendrils, and on both sides of the host leaf.

The egg is between 1/32 and 3/64 inch. Before hatching the egg darkens. It takes 4 - 7 days for the egg to hatch.

The caterpillars feed in groups when young.

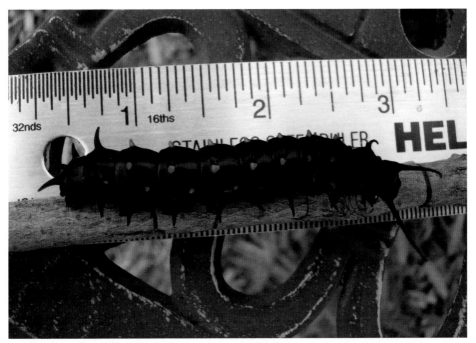

In the last instar, the caterpillar is about 2 1/2 inches. The caterpillar stage is for 15 - 30 days.

Prechrysalis

The chrysalis color can vary.

The chrysalis stage can be as short as 9 days. If it is the last brood, which overwinters, it will not emerge until spring.

Adult Food

They can be found puddling and also feed on Alfalfa, Azalea, Brazilian Verbena, Brodiaeas, Butterfly Bush, Buttonbush, California Buckeye, Cleome, Clover, Firebush, Frostweed, Gilias, Globe Amaranth, Golden Corydalis, Ironweed, Joe-Pye Weed, Lantana, Lilac, Lupine, Mexican Sunflower, Milkweed, Monarda, New England Aster, Pentas, Petunia, Phlox, Porterweed, Sand Verbena, Southern Corydalis, Sunflower, Teasel, Thistle, Viper's Bugloss, Yellow Star Thistle, Yerba Santa, and Zinnia.

Pentas - *Pentas* spp.

Polydamas Swallowtail

Family - Swallowtails - *Papilionidae* (pap-ill-ee-ON-ah-dee)

Flight period: March - December

Polydamas Swallowtail

Polydamas Swallowtail
Battus polydamas (bat-tus • pah-lee-duh-muss)

The wingspan is 2 15/16 - 4 1/16 inches.

The dorsal/upperside is brown with a submarginal pale yellow band.

The ventral/underside is brown. The forewing has a submarginal pale yellow band. The hindwing is brown, has a scalloped margin, and a marginal row of red zigzag spots. This swallowtail is tailless.

Host/Larval Food Plants

Pipevine - *Aristolochia* spp.

Pipevine – *Aristolochia* spp.

They have 2 - 3 broods each year. The eggs are orangish and laid in groups on vines, stems, and tree bark. They are between 1/32 and 3/64 inch.

It takes 5 - 9 days for the egg to hatch.

Young caterpillars feed in groups on the underside of the leaf.

Caterpillars can vary in color. As they mature they become solitary.

The caterpillar stage is for 18 - 24 days.

The chrysalis stage is for 30 - 36 days, except for the last brood, which overwinters.

Adult Food

Some of the flowers they nectar on are: False Heather, Honeysuckle, Lantana, Milkweed, Mistflower, Pentas, Soapweed, and Zinnia.

Spicebush Swallowtail

Family - Swallowtails - *Papilionidae* (pap-ill-ee-ON-ah-dee)

Flight period: April - October, deep south March - December

Spicebush Swallowtail

Spicebush Swallowtail
Papilio troilus (pa-pil-ee-oh • troy-lus)

The wingspan is 3 1/2 - 5 inches.

The dorsal/upperside is black with white spots along the marginal edge of the forewing. The hindwing has iridescent bluish scales on the female and iridescent bluish green scales on the male. There are pale bluish green spots along the marginal edge.

The ventral/underside is black. The forewing is similar to the dorsal. On the hindwing, there are blue scales along the postmedian band with orange spots on either side. The body has rows of white spots.

Host/Larval Food Plants

Camphor Tree - *Cinnamomum camphora*
Sassafras - *Sassafras albidum*
Spicebush - *Lindera benzoin*

Spicebush – *Lindera benzoin*

They have 2 - 3 broods each year. The egg is pale greenish white and laid singly on the underside of the host leaf most of the time.

The egg is between 1/32 and 3/64 inch. Before hatching the egg darkens. It takes 4 - 8 days for the egg to hatch.

When it hatches, the caterpillar is about 3/32 inch.

The first thing it does after hatching is eat its eggshell. Then the caterpillar will use silk it produces to curl a leaf, which it stays in when not eating.

The earlier instars resemble bird droppings and the later instars are snakelike.

In the last instar the caterpillar is yellow and is about 2 3/16 inches. The caterpillar stage is for 16 - 20 days.

The chrysalis stage can be as short as 12 days. If it is the last brood, which overwinters, it will not emerge until spring.

Adult Food

They can be found puddling and also feed on Aster, Azalea, Blazing Star, Brazilian Verbena, Butterfly Bush, Buttonbush, Dogbane, Firebush, French Marigold, Globe Amaranth, Golden Crownbeard, Honeysuckle, Lantana, Lilac, Lupine, Milkweed, Monarda, Pentas, Pineapple Sage, Purple Coneflower, Summer Phlox, Sweet Pepperbush, Thistle, and Zinnia.

Pink Delight Butterfly Bush - *Buddleia davidii*

Cabbage White

Family - White/Sulphur - *Pieridae* (pee-AIR-ri-dee)

Flight period: March - November, all year in the south

Cabbage White

Cabbage White
Pieris rapae (py-er-iss • rap-ee)

The wingspan is 1 3/4 - 2 1/4 inches.

The dorsal/upperside is white. The forewing has a black patch near the apex. The female has two submarginal black spots and the male has one.

The ventral/underside is yellowish green or grayish green.

Host/Larval Food Plants

Broccoli - *Brassica oleracea* spp.
Brussel Sprouts - *Brassica oleracea* spp.
Cabbage – *Brassica oleracea* var. *capitata*
Cauliflower - *Brassica oleracea* spp.
Indian Mustard - *Brassica juncea*
Nasturtium - *Tropaeolum* spp.
Peppergrass - *Lepidium virginicum*
Radish - *Raphanus sativus*
Sweet Alyssum - *Lobularia maritima*

Nasturtium – *Tropaeolum* spp.

They have many broods each year. The egg is laid singly.

32nds

The egg is about 1/64 inch and pale yellowish white. It takes 3 – 7 days for the egg to hatch.

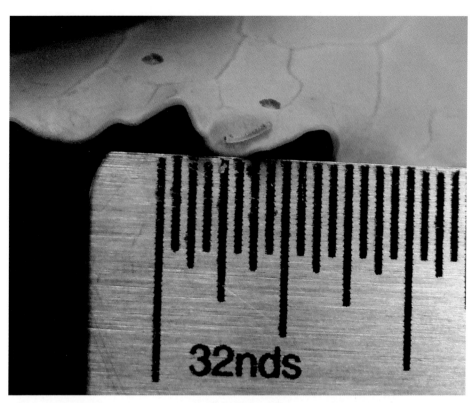

When it hatches, the caterpillar is between 1/16 - 3/32 inch.

The caterpillar stage is for 14 - 20 days. In the last instar, the caterpillar is about 1 3/16 inches.

The caterpillar attaches its rear end to a silk pad and also secures itself with a silk sling around its thorax before making its chrysalis. The chrysalis is jade green at first and then turns yellowish tan.

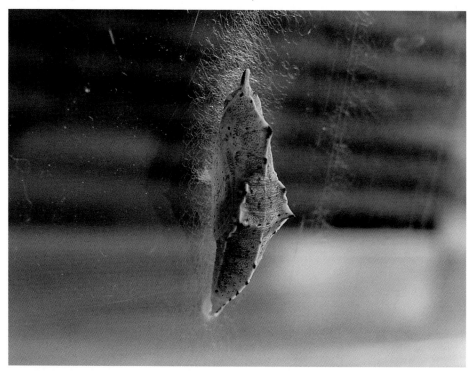

The chrysalis stage is for 8 - 12 days, except for the last brood, which overwinters.

The day before it emerges the chrysalis will become transparent.

Adult Food

Some of the flowers they nectar on are: Aster, Blazingstar, Brazilian Verbena, Butterfly Bush, Coreopsis, Cosmos, Dandelion, Garden Phlox, Joe-Pye Weed, Mint, Mustard, Purple Coneflower, Red Clover, Salvia, Scabiosa, and Scarlet Monkeyflower.

New England Aster - *Symphyotrichum novae-angliae*

Blue Mistflower - *Conoclinium coelestinum*

Great Southern White

Family - White/Sulphur - *Pieridae* (pee-Air-ah-dee)

Flight period: all year deep south

 Great Southern White

Great Southern White
Ascia monuste (ash-ee-ah • mo-nus-te)

The wingspan is 1 13/16 - 3 3/8 inches.

The dorsal/upperside of the male is white. It has a black zigzag on the outer margin. There are two forms of females. One form is similar to the male, except it has wider zigzag markings and a small black cell spot on the forewing. The other has dark scales. Both sexes have turquoise antennal clubs.

The ventral/underside of the male is white or pale yellow. One form of the female is similar to the male. The other is pale brown or smokey gray.

Host/Larval Food Plants

Arugula - *Eruca* spp.
Bayleaf Caper Tree - *Capparis flexuosa*
Cabbage - *Brassica oleracea* var. *capitata*
Caper - *Capparis* spp.
Coastal Searocket - *Cakile lanceolata*
Collard Greens - *Brassica oleracea* var. *acephala*
Garlic Pear Tree - *Crataeva tapia*
Mustard Greens - *Brassica juncea*
Nasturtium - *Tropaeolum* spp.
Peppergrass - *Lepidium virginicum*
Redwhisker Clammyweed - *Polanisia dodecandra*
Saltwort - *Batis maritima*
Tansy Mustard - *Descurainia pinnata brachycarpa*
Watercress - *Nasturtium officinale*

Nasturtium - *Tropaeolum* spp.

They have several broods each year. The eggs are pale yellow and usually laid in groups on the top of the leaf.

The caterpillars have five yellow stripes, separated by mottled gray, that runs the length of the body. All over the body there are tiny and larger black spots.

This caterpillar is on Watercress - *Nasturtium officinale*

In the last instar, the caterpillar is about 2 inches.

Adult Food

Some of the flowers they nectar on are: Butterfly Bush, Coneflower, Daisy, Gumweed, Indian Blanket, Lantana, Milkweed, Mistflower, Saltwort, Salvia, Spanish Needle, Verbena, and Zinnia.

Yellow Lantana - *Lantana* spp.

Clouded Sulphur

Family - White/Sulphur - *Pieridae* (pee-AIR-ri-dee)

Flight period: March - November

Clouded Sulphur

Clouded Sulphur

Colias philodice (co-lee-as • fil-oh-dy-see)

The wingspan is 1 4/5 - 2 3/4 inches.

The dorsal/upperside is yellow. There is a solid black border on the male and an uneven black border with a few yellow spots on the female. Both have a black spot near the top edge of the forewing and a central orange spot on the hindwing. There is also a white form of the female with the same markings as the yellow form.

The ventral/underside is yellow with pink wing edges and a silver spot rimmed with pink on the hindwing.

Host/Larval Food Plants

Alfalfa - *Medicago sativa*
Bush Clover - *Lespedeza* spp.
Red Clover - *Trifolium pratense*
Vetch - *Vicia* spp.
White Clover - *Trifolium repens*
White Sweet Clover - *Melilotus albus*

Red Clover – *Trifolium pratense*

They have several broods each year. The egg is cream and laid singly on the leaf. It turns reddish orange as the caterpillar develops.

The egg is between 1/64 and 1/32 inch and takes 4 - 8 days to hatch.

When it hatches, the caterpillar is about 1/16 inch.

In the last instar, the caterpillar is about 1 3/8 inches. The caterpillar stage is for 14 - 28 days.

Prechrysalis

When the chrysalis is first revealed it is green. It turns yellow as it hardens. Before the butterfly emerges the chrysalis becomes transparent. It is in the chrysalis for as little as 7 days. Since the last brood overwinters, some are in the chrysalis until spring.

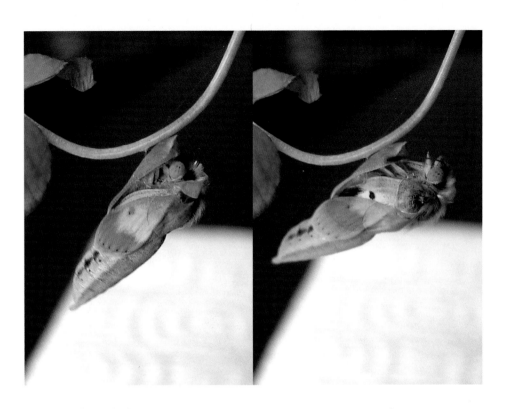

The Clouded Sulphur is emerging from its chrysalis.

Adult Food

They can be found puddling and also feed on Alfalfa, Aster, Blazing Star, Brazilian Verbena, Butterfly Bush, Clover, Dandelion, Dogbane, Garden Phlox, Goldenrod, Hyssop, Marigold, Mexican Sunflower, Milkweed, Mint, Sedum, and Winter Cress.

Marigold – *Tagetes* spp.

Butterfly Bush – *Buddleia davidii*

Eastern Tailed-Blue

Family - Blues - *Lycaenidae* (lie-SEEN-ah-dee)

Flight period: February - November

Eastern Tailed-Blue

Eastern Tailed-Blue
Cupido comyntas (cue-pih-doh • co-min-tahs)

The wingspan is 1/2 - 1 1/8 inches.

The dorsal/upperside of the male is purplish blue and the female is brownish gray. Both sexes have one or two orange spots with a black dot above their tails.

The ventral/underside is pale bluish gray with several blackish gray spots and bands. The hindwing has one to three orange spots with a black dot above their tails.

Host/Larval Food Plants

Alfalfa - *Medicago sativa*
Bush Clover - *Lespedeza* spp.
Clover - *Trifolium* spp.
Lupine - *Lupinus* spp.
Sweet Clover - *Melilotus* spp.
Tick-trefoil - *Desmodium* spp.
Vetch - *Vicia* spp.
Wild Pea - *Lathyrus* spp.

She is laying an egg on Red Clover (*Trifolium pratense*).

They have many broods each year. The egg is laid singly on flowers and young leaves. The egg is pale green.

The egg is about 1/64 inch. It takes 3 - 6 days for the egg to hatch.

When it hatches, the caterpillar is about 3/64 inch. It will feed on buds, flowers, seeds, and young leaves.

Caterpillars vary in color.

The white skin behind it reveals that it has just finished molting. In the last instar, the caterpillar is about 3/8 inch. The caterpillar stage is for 18 - 24 days, except for the last brood, which overwinters in the last instar. It may overwinter in seedpods.

Chrysalises vary in color.

The chrysalis stage is for 3 - 5 days.

The chrysalis becomes transparent before the butterfly emerges.

Adult Food

Males can be found puddling. Some of the plants that they nectar on are: Aster, Brazilian Verbena, Butterfly Bush, Cinquefoil, Dogbane, Goldenrod, Joe-Pye Weed, Milkweed, Mint, Red Clover, Shepherd's Needle, White Sweet Clover, Wild Strawberry, Winter Cress, and Yarrow.

New England Aster - *Symphyotrichum novae-angliae*

Karner Blue

Family - Blues - *Lycaenidae* (lie-SEEN-ah-dee)

Flight period: May - August

Karner Blue

Karner Blue

Lycaeides melissa samuelis (ly-see-ih-dees • me-lis-ah • sam-u-el-is)

The wingspan is about 1 inch.

The dorsal/upperside of the male is silvery or violet blue. It has narrow black margins with white outer fringe. The female is grayish brown with purplish blue near the body and has a row of orange crescents near the edge of the hindwing.

The ventral/underside of both is gray with a row of orange crescents along the wing margins and black spots circled with white.

Host/Larval Food Plants

Wild Lupine - *Lupinus perennis*

Wild Lupine – *Lupinus perennis*

They have 2 broods each year. The egg is laid singly on leaves, stems, and in leaflitter close to the Lupine. It is pale green and slightly larger than 1/32 inch. It takes 5 - 10 days for the egg to hatch. The eggs of the 2nd brood overwinter.

The caterpillar eats the leaf's mexophyll and leaves the epidermis which creates a pattern on the leaf. This is called "window paning". In the last instar, the caterpillar is about 15/16 inch. The caterpillar stage is for 3 - 4 weeks.

The chrysalis stage is for 5 - 12 days.

The adult usually lives 4 - 7 days, but can live up to several weeks.

Adult Food

They can be found puddling and also feed on dung, Aster, Bastard Toad-flax, Bedstraw, Bird's Foot Violet, Black-Eyed Susan, Butterfly Weed, Bachelors Button, Balsam Ragwort, Common Evening Primrose, Common Milkweed, Common Yarrow, Cottonweed, Cream Wild Indigo, Cylindrical Blazing Star, False Spikenard, Fameflower, Fern-Leaved False Foxglove, Flowering Spurge, Frostweed, Goat's Rue, Golden Alexander, Grass-Leaved Goldenrod, Harebell, Hoary Puccoon, Horsemint, Lance-Leaved Coreopsis, Lead Plant, Long-Leaved Bluets, Lyre Leaved Sand Cress, New Jersey Tea, Ohio Spiderwort, Old Field Goldenrod, Pale Spiked Lobelia, Prairie Coreopsis, Prairie Phlox, Purple Milkwort, Purple Prairie Clover, Rough Blazing Star, Round Headed Bush Clover, Showy Goldenrod, Starry False Solomens Seal, Swamp Milkweed, Sweet Everlasting, Thimbleweed, Thyme Leaved Sandwort, Toad Flax, Two Flowered Cynthia, Upland White Aster, Western Sunflower, White Prairie Clover, Whorled Milkweed, Wild Bergamot, Wild Geranium, Wild Lupine, Wild Strawberry, Wood Betony, and Woodland Sunflower.

Wild Geranium - *Geranium maculatum*

Summer Azure

Family - Blues - *Lycaenidae* (lie-SEEN-ah-dee)

Flight period: May - October

Summer Azure

Summer Azure

Celastrina neglecta (sel-ah-stree-nah • ne-glek-tah)

The wingspan is 7/8 - 1 1/4 inches.

The dorsal/upperside is pale blue. The male forewing has a thin dark margin. Its hindwing has a dusting of white scales. The female forewing margin is wider and the hindwing has a greater amount of white scales.

The ventral/underside is chalky white with small dark marks and spots.

Host/Larval Food Plants

Cherry - *Prunus* spp.
Dogwood - *Cornus* spp.
Hog-peanut - *Amphicarpaea bracteata*
Meadowsweet - *Spiraea* spp.
New Jersey Tea - *Ceanothus americanus*
Steeplebush - *Spiraea tomentosa*
Sumac - *Rhus* spp.
Wild Hydrangea - *Hydrangea arborescens*
Wingstem - *Verbesina alternifolia*

New Jersey Tea – *Ceanothus americanus*

They have 1 - 3 broods each year. The egg is laid singly on flower buds and leaf buds. It is greenish white and about 1/32 inch. It takes 3 - 5 days for the egg to hatch.

The caterpillar is sluglike and blends in on the host plant. It feeds on the flowers and buds. A sugary substance, honeydew, is secreted from its dorsal glands. Ants protect the caterpillar from predators and parasites in return for the honeydew.

The caterpillar stage is for 19 - 23 days. In the last instar, the caterpillar is about 19/32 inch.

The chrysalis stage is for 9 - 12 days, except for the last brood which overwinters.

Adult Food

They can be found puddling. Some of the plants they nectar on are: Brazilian Verbena, Blue Mistflower, Clover, Daisy, Dogbane, Dogwood, Joe-Pye Weed, Meadowsweet, Milkweed, New Jersey Tea, Pussytoes, Red Bud, Spirea, Steeplebush, and Sumac.

Joe-Pye Weed - *Eupatorium maculatum*

American Lady

Family - Brushfoots - *Nymphalidae* (nim-FAL-ah-dee)

Flight period: April - November, all year deep south

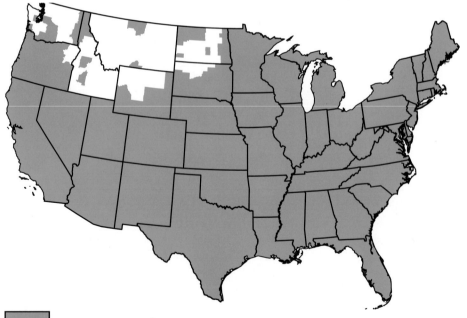

American Lady

American Lady
Vanessa virginiensis (van-ess-ah • ver-jin-ee-in-sis)

The wingspan is 1 3/4 - 2 5/8 inches.

The dorsal/upperside is mainly orange. The forewing has black marks and white spots near the apex. The hindwing has a black band and black marks near the outer margin. Near the submarginal area there are four black spots. The two outer spots have blue in the middle.

The ventral/underside is brown with a cream cobweb pattern. There are two large eyespots on the hindwing, pink markings on the forewing, and a narrow lavender band near the outer margins.

Host/Larval Food Plants

Burdock – *Arctium lappa*
Curry Plant - *Helichrysum angustifolium*
Ironweed – *Vernonia* spp.
Pearly Everlasting – *Anaphalis margaritacea*
Pussytoes – *Antennaria* spp.
Silver Brocade – *Artemisia stelleriana*
Sweet Everlasting – *Pseudognaphalium obtusifolium*

Pearly Everlasting – *Anaphalis margaritacea*

Silver Brocade – *Artemisia stelleriana*

They have 3 - 4 broods each year. Usually the eggs are laid singly but sometimes you will see a couple together.

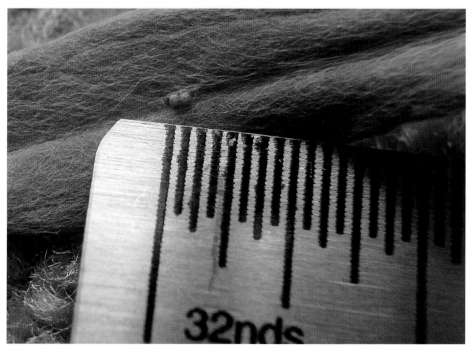

The egg is about 1/64 inch and pale yellowish green. It takes 3 – 6 days for the egg to hatch.

When it hatches, the caterpillar is between 1/16 – 3/32 inch.

The caterpillar encloses itself in the leaves, of which it eats, with silk for protection.

The caterpillars's appearance can vary.

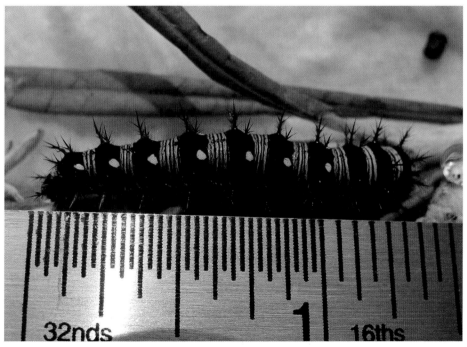

The caterpillar stage is for 18 – 22 days. In the last instar, the caterpillar is about 1 5/8 inches.

It will hang in J for about 24 hours before making its chrysalis.

The chrysalis stage is for 8 – 12 days. The day before it emerges the chrysalis becomes transparent.

Adult Food

Aster, Black-eyed Susan, Brazilian Verbena, Butterfly Bush, Coreopsis, Dogbane, Goldenrod, Heliotrope, Hyssop, Indian Hemp, Marigold, Milkweed, Phlox, Purple Coneflower, Scabiosa, Selfheal, Vetch, Yarrow, Zinnia

Black-eyed Susan – *Rudbeckia* spp.

Butterfly Bush – *Buddleia davidii*

Baltimore Checkerspot

Family - Brushfoots - *Nymphalidae* (nim-FAL-ah-dee)

Flight period: May - August

Baltimore Checkerspot

Baltimore Checkerspot

Euphydryas phaeton (u-fee-dry-as • fay-ton)

The wingspan is 1 3/4 - 2 3/4 inches.

The dorsal/upperside is black with several rows of cream white spots towards the outer edge, a row of reddish orange spots along the outer wing margins, and reddish orange spots towards the base.

The ventral/underside has orange spots along the outer edge, then several rows of cream white spots. Closer to the basal area there is a mixture of orange and white spots.

Host/Larval Food Plants

They have 1 brood each year. The eggs are about 1/32 inch and laid in a mass. When first laid the eggs are yellow. In a couple of days they turn light orange, then reddish. It takes about 2 - 3 weeks for the eggs to hatch. After they hatch the caterpillars build a silken bag-like nest which they eat communally inside of. They overwinter in the 4th instar.

Before overwintering they use these plants:

English Plantain - *Plantago lanceolata*
Hairy Beardtongue - *Penstemon hirsutus*
Turtlehead - *Chelone glabra*
Yellow False Foxglove - *Aureolaria* spp.

Turtlehead - *Chelone glabra*

In the spring they wander off and feed solitarily.

After overwintering they may also feed on these:

Honeysuckle - *Lonicera* spp.
Lousewort - *Pedicularis canadensis*
Viburnum - *Viburnum* spp.
White Ash - *Fraxinus americana*

Arrowwood Viburnum - *Viburnum dentatum*

The caterpillar stage is for 10 - 14 days. In the last instar, the caterpillar is about 1 3/4 inches.

The chrysalis stage is for 9 - 12 days.

Adult Food

Some flowers they nectar on are: Dogbane, Indian Blanket, Lobelia, Milkweed, Purple Coneflower, Swamp Thistle, Viburnum, and Wild Rose.

Common Buckeye

Family - Brushfoots - *Nymphalidae* (nim-FAL-ah-dee)

Flight period: May - October, all year deep south

Common Buckeye

Common Buckeye

Junonia coenia (joo-no-nee-ah • see-nee-ah)

The wingspan is 1 1/2 - 2 3/4 inches.

The dorsal/upperside is brown. The forewing has two eyespots, a white patch, and two small orange bars. The hindwing has two eyespots, a light brownish border, and an orange margin just inside of the border.

The ventral/underside of the forewing and hindwing is similar to the dorsal, except it is a duller version.

Host/Larval Food Plants

American Blueheart - *Buchnera americana*
Butter and Eggs - *Linaria vulgaris*
False Foxglove - *Agalinis* spp.
Firecracker - *Russelia* spp.
Fogfruit - *Phyla* spp.
Green Shrimp - *Blechum pyramidatum*
Indian Paintbrush - *Castilleja* spp.
Plantain - *Plantago* spp.
Snapdragon - *Antirrhinum* spp.
Snapdragon Vine - *Maurandya antirrhiniflora*
Sticky Monkeyflower - *Mimulus aurantiacus*
Toadflax - *Linaria* spp.
Twinflower - *Dyschoriste oblongifolia*
Wild Petunia - *Ruellia* spp.
Yaupon Blacksenna - *Seymeria cassioides*

Yaupon Blacksenna - *Seymeria cassioides*

English Plantain - *Plantago lanceolata*

Butter and Eggs - *Linaria vulgaris*

They have several broods each year. Usually the eggs are laid singly but sometimes you will see a couple together.

The egg is between 1/64 and 1/32 inch and green. It takes 3 – 6 days for the egg to hatch.

When it hatches, the caterpillar is about 1/16 inch.

The caterpillar stage is for 12 - 16 days. In the last instar, the caterpillar is about 1 3/4 inches.

The caterpillar attaches to a silk pad with its cremaster. It then hangs for about 24 hours before making its chrysalis.

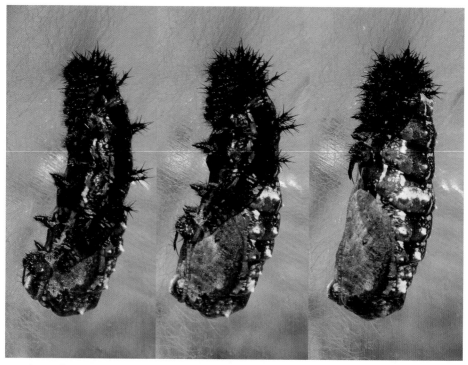

It takes about 1 minute to make its chrysalis.

The chrysalis stage is for 7 - 10 days, except for the last brood in the south, which overwinters.

Shortly before the butterfly emerges from the chrysalis it becomes slightly transparent.

The adult lives about 10 days, except for those which overwinter in the south.

The Common Buckeye is sunning itself.

Red Clover - *Trifolium pratense*

Adult Food

They often can be seen puddling and also feed on carrion, dung, rotten fruit, Aster, Brazilian Verbena, Butterfly Bush, California Buckwheat, Chickory, Clover, Cosmos, Dogbane, Frogfruit, Gumweed, Knapweed, Lantana, Milkweed, Peppermint, and Tickseed Sunflower.

Gumweed - *Grindelia* spp.

Common Wood Nymph

Family - Brushfoots - *Nymphalidae* (nim-FAL-ah-dee)

Flight period: May - October

Common Wood Nymph

Common Wood Nymph
Cercyonis pegala (ser-see-oh-nis • peg-ah-la)

The wingspan is 1 7/8 - 3 inches.

The dorsal/upperside is dark brown with two black eyespots encircling a small white spot on the forewing. Some have a yellow patch around the eyespots.

The ventral/underside is brown. Some have a yellow patch around the eyespots and a small white dot within. There are several small eyespots on the hindwing.

Host/Larval Food Plants

Many grasses, some are:
Beardgrass - *Bothriochloa* spp.
Bluegrass - *Poa* spp.
Bluestem - *Andropogon* - spp.
Purpletop Tridens - *Tridens flavus*
Wild Oat - *Avena fatua*

Big Bluestem - *Andropogon gerardii*

They have 1 brood each year. The eggs are pale yellow or white. They lay the eggs singly on or near the host plant. As it develops the egg will change to tan, then orangish brown or pinkish mottling.

When the caterpillar hatches it does not eat. Instead it goes into hibernation. The following year it will complete its life cycle.

In the last instar, the caterpillar is about 2 inches.

Adult Food

They can be found puddling and also feed on dung, fungi, rotten fruit, tree sap, Alfalfa, Aster, Blue Vervain, Boneset, Brazilian Verbena, Butterfly Bush, Button Bush, Cherry Blossoms, Clover, Fleabane, Goldenrod, Hyssop, Ironweed, Joe-Pye Weed, Lantana, Milkweed, Mint, Monarda, Purple Coneflower, Sunflower, and Thistle.

Eastern Comma

Family - Brushfoots - *Nymphalidae* (nim-FAL-ah-dee)

Flight period: March - October

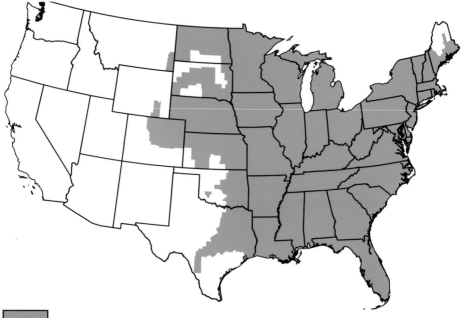

Eastern Comma

Eastern Comma

Polygonia comma (pol-ih-go-nee-ah • com-ah)

The wingspan is 1 3/4 - 2 1/2 inches.

The dorsal/upperside of the forewing is orange with black spots and borders. The hindwing of the summer form is mostly black, the winter form is mostly orange.

The ventral/underside looks like a dead leaf. The hindwing has a curved silvery spot that resembles a comma.

Host/Larval Food Plants

Elm - *Ulmus* spp.
False Nettle - *Boehmeria cylindrica*
Hackberry - *Celtis* spp.
Hops - *Humulus* spp.
Nettle - *Urtica* spp.
Wood Nettle - *Laportea canadensis*

False Nettle - *Boehmeria cylindrica*

Common Hop - *Humulus lupulus*

They have 2 broods each year. The eggs are green and laid singly or stacked.

The egg is between 1/64 - 1/32 inch. As the caterpillar develops the egg darkens. It takes 4 – 6 days for the egg to hatch.

The caterpillars usually eat at night. Older caterpillars make shelters by stitching the leaf edges together with silk. Their color can vary.

The caterpillar stage is for 19 - 22 days. The second brood are usually in the caterpillar stage longer. In the last instar, the caterpillar is about 1 9/16 inches.

The caterpillar is hanging in J.

The chrysalis stage is for 7 - 11 days.

Some adults of the winter form will overwinter. They will use hollow logs, wood piles, cervices of trees, earthen crevices, under bark, or under shingles to hibernate in. Others will migrate south for the winter. On warm sunny days in the winter they may be seen flying around. The adults can live up to 8 months.

Adult Food

They are often seen puddling and also feed on dung, rotting fruit, tree sap, Butterfly Bush, Dandelion, Joe-Pye Weed, Milkweed, Purple Coneflower, Showy Stonecrop, and Smooth Sumac.

Great Spangled Fritillary

Family - Brushfoots - *Nymphalidae* (nim-FAL-ah-dee)

Flight period: June - September

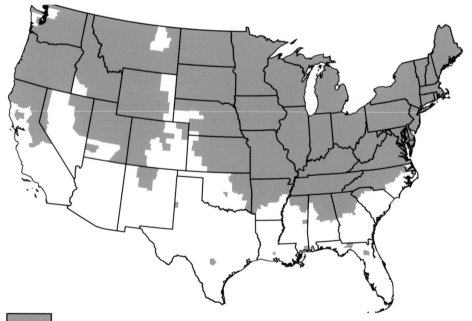

▨ Great Spangled Fritillary

Great Spangled Fritillary
Speyeria cybele (spay-er-ee-ah • sib-el-ee)

The wingspan is 2 1/2 - 4 inches.

The dorsal/upperside is orange with heavy black lines and spots.

The ventral/underside of the forewing is similar to the dorsal. The hindwing is orange with metallic silver spots and a yellowish submarginal band.

Host/Larval Food Plants

Violet - *Viola* spp.

Violet - *Viola* spp.

They have 1 brood each year.

The female will walk under the violets as she deposits her eggs. Only a few may actually end up on the plants. Most will be near them.

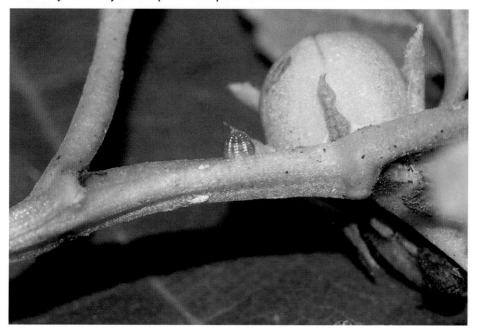

As the egg develops it darkens. The egg stage is for 3 - 4 days.

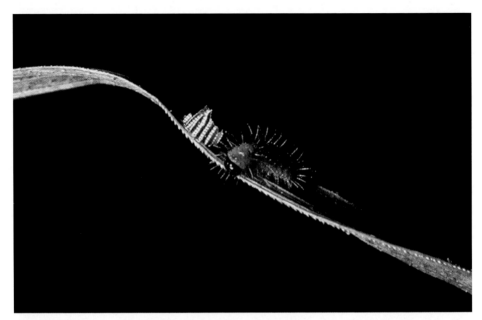

When the caterpillar hatches from the egg the only thing that it will consume, other than its eggshell, is water. It will then overwinter.

In the spring when the violets begin to grow the caterpillar will come out of hibernation.

The caterpillar will then start eating, which it only does at night, and complete its life cycle.

In the last instar, the caterpillar is about 2 3/16 inches.

The chrysalis stage is for 9 - 18 days.

Adult Food

Some of the flowers they nectar on are: Blazing Star, Butterfly Bush, Coreopsis, Dogbane, Ironweed, Joe-Pye Weed, Lantana, Lavender, Mexican Sunflower, Milkweed, Monarda, Mountain Laurel, Purple Coneflower, Red Clover, Thistle, Verbena, Vetch, White Snakeroot, and Zinnia.

Butterfly Bush - *Buddleia davidii*

Gulf Fritillary

Family - Brushfoots - *Nymphalidae* (nim-FAL-ah-dee)

Flight period: March - November, all year deep south

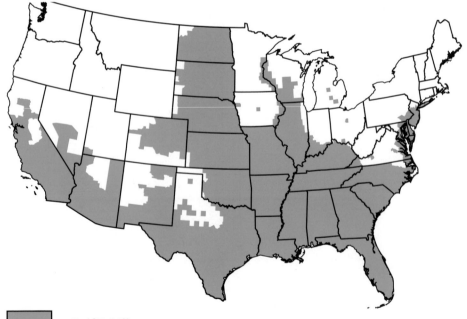

Gulf Fritillary

Gulf Fritillary

Agraulis vanillae (a-grau-liss • va-nil-lee)

The wingspan is 2 1/2 - 3 3/4 inches.

The dorsal/upperside is bright orange with black markings. There are three small white spots outlined with black on the forewings.

The ventral/underside is brown or brownish orange with orange at the base of the forewings. There are elongated silvery spots on the hindwings and also on the edge of the forewings.

Host/Larval Food Plants

Passion-vine – *Passiflora* spp.

Passion-vine – *Passiflora* spp.

Passion-vine - *Passiflora* spp.

They have several broods each year. The eggs are yellow and laid singly on the leaves or tendrils. As the caterpillar develops the egg turns a reddish brown. It takes 4 - 8 days for the egg to hatch.

Their appearance can vary. In the last instar, it is about 1 3/4 inches. The caterpillar stage can be as little as 10 days or more than 48 days.

152   Brushfoots

The caterpillar is hanging in J.   It is in the chrysalis for 5 -10 days.

Adult Food

They feed on carrion, dung, Aster, Butterfly Bush, Cordia, Cowpen Daisy, Drummond Phlox, False Heather, Firebush, Goldeneye, Hibiscus, Lantana, Mexican Flame Vine, Pentas, Porterweed, Shepherd's Needle, Spanish Needles, Stokes Aster, Thistle, Tread Softly, Verbena, and Zinnia.

The adult lives up to 6 months and overwinters in the south.

Julia Heliconian

Family - Brushfoots - *Nymphalidae* (nim-FAL-ah-dee)

Flight period: all year deep south

Julia Heliconian

Julia Heliconian
Dryas iulia (dry-as • u-lee-ah)

The wingspan is 3 - 3 5/8 inches.

The dorsal/upperside of the male is bright orange with black spots towards the apex. The female is dull orange with a black bar across the apex. The hindwing of the male and female has a narrow black margin.

The ventral/underside is light brownish orange with a pale band through the center.

Host/Larval Food Plants

Passion-vine – *Passiflora* spp.

Passion-vine – *Passiflora* spp.

She is laying an egg.

They have several broods each year. The eggs are yellow and laid singly. The female prefers to lay eggs in shady locations.

In the last instar, the caterpillar is about 1 3/4 inches.

Chrysalis

Adult Food

They can be found puddling and also feed on pollen, Brazilian Verbena, Butterfly Bush, Coneflower, Firebush, Ghost Plant, Lantana, Largeflower Mexican Clover, Mexican Sunflower, Mistflower, Pentas, Porterweed, Spanish Needles, White Beggar-Ticks, and Zinnia.

Firebush - *Hamelia patens*

Monarch

Family - Brushfoots - *Nymphalidae* (nim-FAL-ah-dee)

Flight period: March - November, all year deep south

Monarch

Monarch

Danaus plexippus (dan-ay-us • plex-ih-pus)

The wingspan is 3 1/2 - 4 inches.

The dorsal/upperside is orange with black veins and a black border that contains two rows of white spots. The forewing has white spots near the apex. The hindwing of the female has thick veins. The male has thin veins with a black scent patch near the inner margin.

The ventral/underside is similar to the dorsal, except it is lighter orange.

Host/Larval Food Plants

Milkweed - *Asclepias* spp.

Butterfly Weed – *Asclepias tuberosa*

Swamp Milkweed – *Asclepias incarnata*

They have several broods each year. The eggs are ivory and laid singly under the leaves and sometimes on top of the leaves.

They are also laid on the flower buds.

The egg is about 1/32 inch.

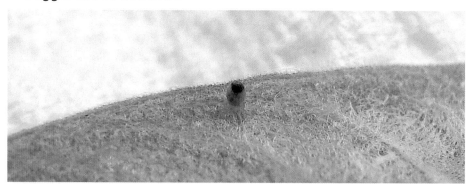

It takes 3 – 6 days for the egg to hatch. One day before emerging from the egg its black head is visible.

Most or all of the eggshell is eaten by the caterpillar after hatching.

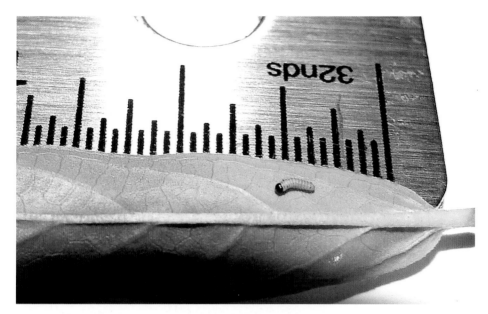

When it hatches, the caterpillar is about 3/32 inch.

Monarch caterpillars have 5 instars. This one has just finished molting. You can see the head capsule (to the right), which comes off first, and the skin it just crawled out of (to the left). Its antennae are still folded in half and the new head capsule is a light color. Shortly the antennae will straighten up and the head capsule will darken. After the caterpillar's new skin dries it will turn around and eat the old skin.

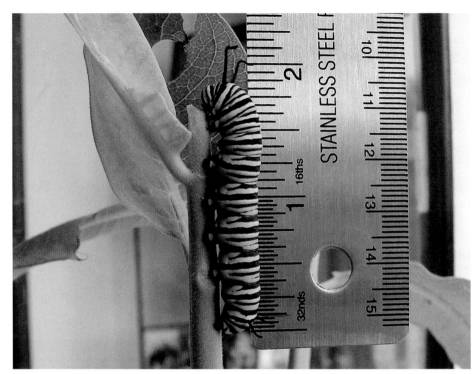

The caterpillar stage is for 9 - 16 days. In the last instar, the caterpillar is about 2 inches.

The caterpillar will hang in J for about 24 hours before making its chrysalis. Right before it molts for the last time it will hang straight down. The skin will split behind its head and the molting then begins.

It takes less than 2 minutes to reveal its chrysalis.

As the chrysalis hardens it becomes smooth and jade green with metallic gold spots. It will be in the chrysalis stage for 9 - 14 days. The day before it emerges the chrysalis will become transparent.

About 15 minutes after the Monarch begins to come out of the chrysalis the wings are completely expanded. It takes several hours for the wings to harden and dry.

Adult Food

Aster, Blazing Star, Bougainvillea, Butterfly Bush, Buttonbush, Clover, Cosmos, Eucalyptus, Garden Phlox, Goldenrod, Golden Dewdrop, Hyssop, Ironweed, Joe-Pye Weed, Lantana, Mexican Plum, Mexican Sunflower, Milkweed, Pentas, Purple Coneflower, Verbena, Thistle, and Zinnia.

Mexican Sunflower – *Tithonia rotundifolia*

New England Aster – *Symphyotrichum novae-angliae*

Mourning Cloak

Family - Brushfoots - *Nymphalidae* (nim-FAL-ah-dee)

Flight period: March - October, all year in the south

Mourning Cloak

Mourning Cloak
Nymphalis antiopa (nim-fal-iss • an-tee-oh-pa)

The wingspan is 3 - 4 inches.

The dorsal/upperside is purplish black with a board yellow border and a row of iridescent blue spots just inside of the border.

The ventral/underside is dark brown and bark like in appearance with a yellowish border.

Host/Larval Food Plants

Elm - *Ulmus* spp.
Hackberry - *Celtis* spp.
Paper Birch - *Betula papyrifera*
Poplar - *Populus* spp.
Sugarberry - *Celtis laevigata*
Willow - *Salix* spp.

Black Willow - *Salix nigra*

They have 1 or perhaps 2 broods each year. The eggs are laid in clusters around twigs and on leaves of the host plant. They are pale olive green with white ridges when first laid. As they develop they turn red and then black. The eggs are slightly larger than 1/32 inch. It takes 10 - 14 days for the eggs to hatch.

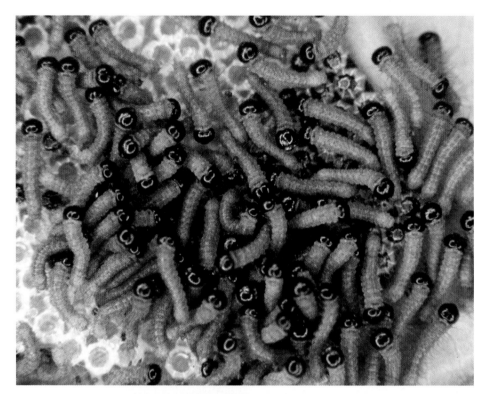

The caterpillars stay together until they are full grown. At that time they will leave the host plant in search for a place to make their chrysalis.

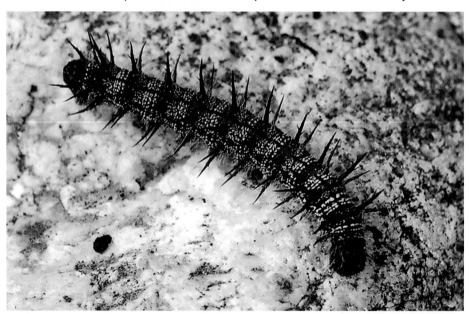

The caterpillar stage is for 14- 18 days. In the last instar, the caterpillar is about 2 3/16 inches.

The chrysalis stage is for 8 - 15 days.

The adult overwinters in tree crevices, hollow logs, and other sheltered spots. They can be seen on warm sunny winter days. In the summer they may aestivate during the hottest months. They can live up to 12 months.

Adult Food

They prefer dung, rotting fruit, and tree sap but will also feed on Andromeda Bush, Brazilian Verbena, Butterfly Bush, Cherry Blossoms, Coneflower, Dogbane, Goldenrod, Lantana, Lilac, Manzanita, Milkweed, New Jersey Tea, Pussy Willow Flowers, and Shasta Daisy.

Painted Lady

Family - Brushfoots - *Nymphalidae* (nim-FAL-ah-dee)

Flight period: May to October, all year in the south

Painted Lady

Painted Lady
Vanessa cardui (van-ess-ah • car-du-i)

The wingspan is 1 3/4 - 2 1/2 inches.

The dorsal/upperside is mainly orange with black marks and white spots near the apex of the forewing. The hindwing has black marks and three rows of black spots near the outer margin.

The ventral/underside is brown with a cream cobweb pattern. The forewing has pink markings. The hindwing has a row of small blue marks between the margin and the four small eyespots.

Host/Larval Food Plants

Borage - *Borago officinalis*
Hollyhock - *Alcea* spp.
Mallow - *Malva* spp.
Sunflower - *Helianthus* spp.
Thistle - *Cirsium* spp.
Tree Mallow - *Lavatera maritima*

Mallow – *Malva* spp.

She is laying an egg on Thistle – *Cirsium* spp.

They have several broods each year. The eggs are between 1/64 and 1/32 inch. They are light aqua and laid singly.

It takes 5 – 9 days for the egg to hatch. The day before emerging the egg turns dark revealing the caterpillar.

When it hatches, the caterpillar is between 1/16 and 3/32 inch.

The caterpillar encloses itself in a silkened nest, within the leaves, for protection while it eats.

The caterpillar stage is for 12 - 18 days. In the last instar, the caterpillar is about 1 5/8 inches.

The caterpillar will hang in J for about 24 hours before making its chrysalis. It will be in the chrysalis for 9 - 14 days. The day before it emerges the chrysalis will become transparent.

Adult Food

Some of the flowers they nectar on are: Anchor Plant, Aster, Blazing Star, Brazilian Verbena, Butterfly Bush, Buttonbush, California Buckwheat, Coreopsis, Cosmos, Escallonia, Ironweed, Joe-Pye Weed, Lantana, Mexican Sunflower, Milkweed, New England Aster, Privet, Purple Coneflower, Red Clover, Scabiosa, Scarlet Monkeyflower, Thistle, and Zinnia.

Sand Coreopsis - *Coreopsis lanceolata*

Pearl Crescent

Family - Brushfoots - *Nymphalidae* (nim-FAL-ah-dee)

Flight period: April - November, all year deep south.

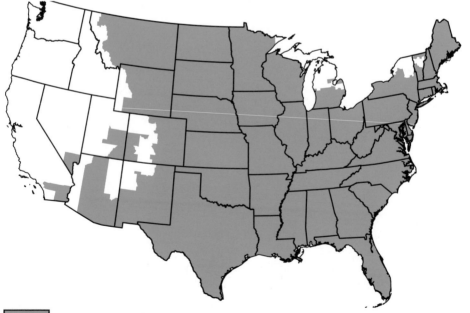

Pearl Crescent

Pearl Crescent
Phyciodes tharos (fy-see-oh-dees • thar-ohs)

The wingspan is 1 1/4 - 1 5/8 inches.

The dorsal/upperside is orange with a lacelike pattern made with thin black lines. It has black wing borders and a row of small spots near the border of the hindwing. The female is larger than the male and is darker with white markings on the forewings.

The ventral/underside is mottled with a dark marginal patch consisting of a silvery crescent.

Host/Larval Food Plants

Aster - *Symphyotrichum* spp.

Smooth Blue Aster - *Symphyotrichum laevis*

New England Aster - *Symphyotrichum novae-angliae*

She is laying eggs.

They have several broods each year. The eggs are pale green and laid in small clusters on the underside of the host leaf. It takes 4 - 6 days for the eggs to hatch.

In the last instar, the caterpillar is about 3/4 inch. The caterpillar stage is for 10 - 12 days, except for the last brood which overwinters.

The chrysalis stage is for 7 - 12 days.

Adult Food

Some of the flowers they nectar on are: Aster, Black-eyed Susan, Butterfly Bush, Butterfly Weed, Dogbane, Frostweed, Joe-Pye Weed, Mexican Sunflower, Milkweed, Obedient Plant, Orange Coneflower, Purple Coneflower, Shepherd's Needle, Snow-on-the-Mountain, Thistle, and Winter Cress.

Butterfly Weed - *Asclepias tuberosa*

Queen

Family - Brushfoots - *Nymphalidae* (nim-FAL-ah-dee)

Flight period: April - November, all year deep south

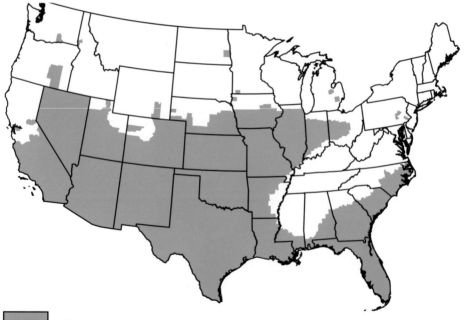

Queen

Queen

Danaus gilippus (dan-ay-us • gil-ih-pus)

The wingspan is 2 5/8 - 3 3/4 inches.

The dorsal/upperside is mahogany with white spots in the black wing margins. The forewing has white spots in the postmedian and subapical. The male has a black scent patch along the inner margin.

The ventral/underside is similar to the dorsal, except the hindwing has black veins.

Host/Larval Food Plants

Bearded Swallow-wort - *Cynanchum barbigerum*
Blodgett's Swallow-wort - *Cynanchum blodgettii*
Climbing Milkweed - *Sarcostemma* spp.
Milkweed - *Asclepias* spp.
White Twinevine - *Sarcostemma clausum*

Bloodflower – *Asclepias curassavica*

They have several broods each year. The eggs are about 1/32 inch. They are white and laid singly on leaves, stems, and flower buds.

It takes 4 - 6 days for the egg to hatch.

The caterpillar has three pair of black filaments. The caterpillar stage is 14 - 16 days. In the last instar, the caterpillar is about 2 inches.

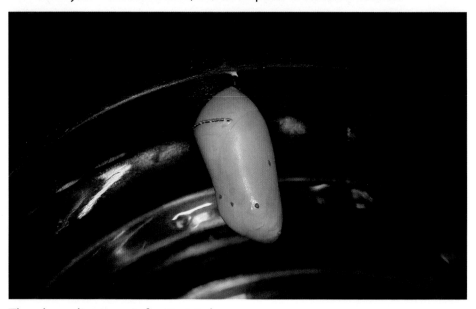

The chrysalis stage is for 9 - 11 days.

Adult Food

Certain flowers have alkaloids (chemical compounds) that are required for breeding. The males will seek these out. Some of these are in the genera Ageratum, Eupatorium, and Heliotropium.

Some of the flowers they nectar on are: Aster, Butterfly Bush, Coneflower, Fogfruit, Ghost Plant, Goldenrod, Gumweed, Heliotrope, Hibiscus, Mexican Sunflower, Milkweed, Mistflower, Pentas, Porterweed, Spanish Needles, St. John's Wort, Starflower, Thistle, Threadleaf Groundsel, Verbena, White Twinevine, Wild Tamarind, and Zinnia.

Hibiscus - *Hibiscus* - spp.

Question Mark

Family - Brushfoots - *Nymphalidae* (nim-FAL-ah-dee)

Flight period: April - November

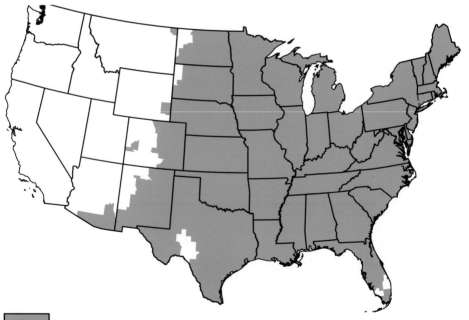

Question Mark

Question Mark

Polygonia interrogationis (pol-ih-go-nee-ah • in-ter-oh-gat-ee-oh-nis)

The wingspan is 2 1/4 - 3 inches.

The dorsal/upperside of the forewing is orange with brownish black spots. It is similar to the Eastern Comma, except it has an extra mark above the three spots that are in a row, and it is larger. The hindwing of the summer form is mostly black and the winter form is mostly orange.

The ventral/underside looks like a dead leaf. There is a silvery spot on the hindwing that resembles a question mark.

Host/Larval Food Plants

Elm - *Ulmus* spp.
False Nettle - *Boehmeria cylindrica*
Hackberry - *Celtis* spp.
Hops - *Humulus* spp.
Nettle - *Urtica* spp.
Sugarberry - *Celtis laevigata*

Common Hop – *Humulus lupulus*

They have 2 broods each year. The eggs are green and laid singly, in small groups, or stacked. They lay the eggs on the host plant, and they also lay them on the ground, on a plant, or an object that is close to the host plant. If the egg is not on the host plant when the caterpillar emerges, it must seek it out.

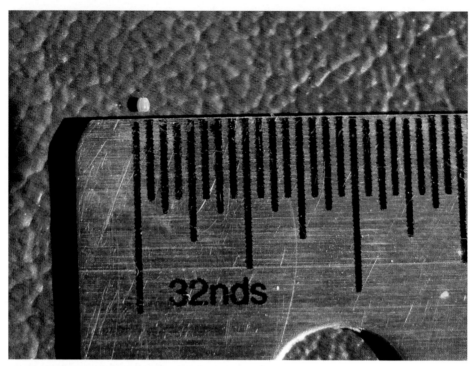

The egg is between 1/64 - 1/32 inch.

The egg darkens as the caterpillar develops. It takes 3 – 7 days for the egg to hatch.

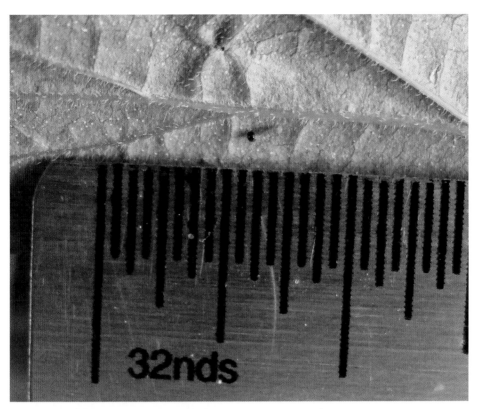

When it hatches, the caterpillar is about 1/16 inch.

The caterpillars can be found underneath the leaves of the host plant.

The caterpillar's appearance can vary.

The caterpillar stage is for 14 - 18 days. In the last instar, the caterpillar is about 1 3/4 inches.

The caterpillar is hanging in J.

The caterpillar is molting for the last time as it reveals its chrysalis. It is in the chrysalis for 7 - 10 days.

The adult can live up to 8 months. It overwinters in hollow logs, wood piles, cervices of trees, earthen crevices, under bark, and under shingles.

Adult Food

They prefer carrion, dung, puddling, rotting fruit, and tree sap, but will also feed on Aster, Butterfly Bush, Purple Coneflower, Milkweed, and Sweet Pepperbush.

Purple Coneflower - *Echinacea purpurea*

The Question Marks are feeding on overripe fruit.

Red Admiral

Family - Brushfoots - *Nymphalidae* (nim-FAL-ah-dee)

Flight period: March - November, all year deep south

Red Admiral

Red Admiral

Vanessa atalanta (van-ess-ah • at-ah-lan-tah)

The wingspan is 1 3/4 - 2 1/2 inches.

The dorsal/upperside is black. The forewing has reddish orange bands and small white spots near the apex. The hindwing has a reddish orange border.

The ventral/underside of the forewing is similar to the dorsal side. The hindwing is mottled and lacks the reddish orange border.

Host/Larval Food Plants

False Nettle - *Boehmeria cylindrica*
Mamaki - *Pipturus albidus*
Nettle - *Urtica* spp.
Pennsylvania Pellitory - *Parietaria pensylvanica*
Wood Nettle - *Laportea canadensis*

False Nettle – *Boehmeria cylindrica*

They have several broods each year. The eggs are green, laid singly, and measure between 1/64 - 1/32 inch. It takes 3 - 6 days for the egg to hatch.

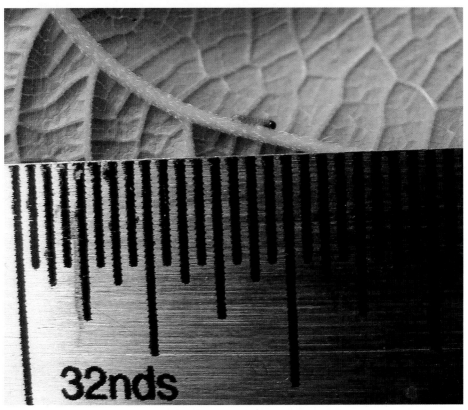

When it hatches, the caterpillar is about 1/16 inch. For protection it stitches the leaf closed and eats the leaf from within.

The caterpillar stage is for 14 - 21 days. In the last instar, the caterpillar is about 1 1/2 inches.

The caterpillar will hang in J for about 24 hours before making its chrysalis.

The chrysalis stage is for 8 - 12 days.

The chrysalis becomes transparent the day before the butterfly emerges.

Adult Food

They can be found puddling and also feed on dung, rotting fruit, salts from human perspiration, and tree sap.

Some of the flowers they nectar on are: Alfalfa, Anchor Plant, Aster, Bougainvillea, Brazilian Verbena, Butterfly Bush, Choke Cherry, Purple Coneflower, Crab Apple, Creeping Phlox, Escallonia, Golden Dewdrop, Lantana, Lilac, Milkweed, Pentas, Red Clover, Saliva, and Sedum.

Purple Coneflower – *Echinacea purpurea*

"Ice Ballet" Swamp Milkweed – *Asclepias incarnata*

Butterfly Weed – *Asclepias tuberosa*

Red-spotted Purple

Family - Brushfoots - *Nymphalidae* (nim-FAL-ah-dee)

Flight period: April - October

Red-spotted Purple

Red-spotted Purple
Limenitis arthemis (le-men-ee-tis • ar-thee-mis)

The wingspan is 3 - 3 1/2 inches.

The dorsal/upperside is mainly purplish blue with iridescent blue on the outer portion of the hindwing.

The ventral/underside is brownish black with reddish orange spots near the base and a row of orange spots near the outer edge.

Host/Larval Food Plants

Apple - *Malus* spp.
Aspen - *Populus* spp.
Basswood - *Tilia* spp.
Birch - *Betulaceae* spp.
Cherry - *Prunus* spp.
Cottonwood - *Populus* spp.
Deerberry - *Vaccinium stamineum*
Hawthorn - *Crataegus* spp.
Hornbeam - *Carpinus caroliniana*
Oak - *Quercus* spp.
Pear - *Pyrus* spp.
Poplar - *Populus* spp.
Shadbush - *Amelanchier* spp.
Willow - *Salix* spp.

Wild Black Cherry – *Prunus serotina*

Corkscrew Willow - *Salix matsudana* and Pussy Willow – *Salix discolor*

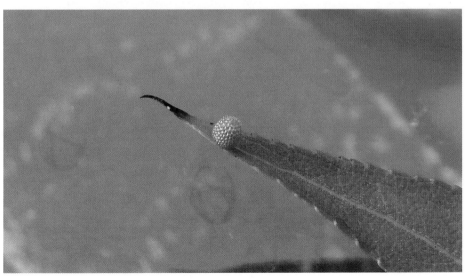

They have 2 broods each year. The eggs are grayish green and laid singly on the tip of the host leaf.

The egg is about 1/32 inch.

The egg darkens as the caterpillar develops. It takes 4 – 8 days for the egg to hatch.

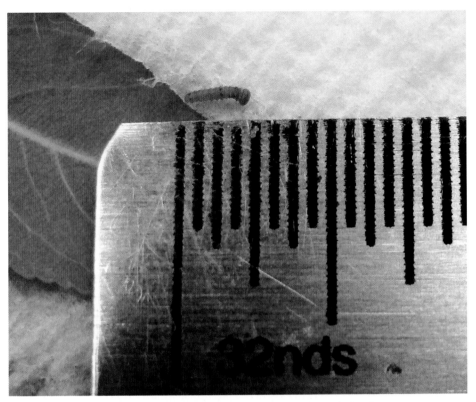

When it hatches, the caterpillar is between 3/32 - 1/8 inch.

The caterpillar often eats around the vein of the leaf.

The caterpillar has just finished molting. Its old skin is behind it. The new head capsule and spined horns are a light color. Shortly they will darken.

The 3rd instar of the last brood overwinters in a hibernaculum. To make the hibernaculum it first attaches the leaf to the twig with silk. Then it stitches the leaf together with silk and crawls in.

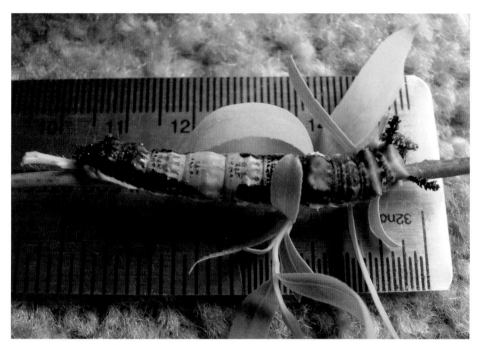

The caterpillar stage is for 21 - 28 days, except for the last brood, which overwinters. In the last instar, the caterpillar is about 2 inches.

The caterpillar will hang in J before making its chrysalis.

The chrysalis stage is for 6 - 12 days.

Adult Food

Some of the things they feed on are: aphid honeydew, carrion, dung, rotting fruit, spittle of spittlebugs on Goldenrods, tree sap, Brazilian Verbena, Butterfly Bush, Dogbane, Lantana, Milkweed, Pentas, Privet, Purple Coneflower, Spiraea, Staghorn, Sumac, Thistle, and Viburnum.

Purple Coneflower – *Echinacea purpurea*

Pink Delight Butterfly Bush – *Buddleia davidii*

The Red-spotted Purple is feeding on a banana.

Viceroy

Family - Brushfoots - *Nymphalidae* (nim-FAL-ah-dee)

Flight period: April - October, all year Florida

Viceroy

Viceroy

Limenitis archippus (le-min-ee-tis • ar-kip-us)

The wingspan is 2 1/2 - 3 1/4 inches.

The dorsal/upperside is orange with black veins and a black border that contains two rows of white spots. The forewing has a black postmedian line and white spots. The hindwing has a black postmedian line.

The ventral/underside is similar to the dorsal, except it is a lighter orange and has larger white spots.

Host/Larval Food Plants

Aspen - *Populus* spp.
Cottonwood - *Populus deltoides*
Poplar - *Populus* spp.
Willow - *Salix* spp.

Cottonwood – *Populus deltoides*

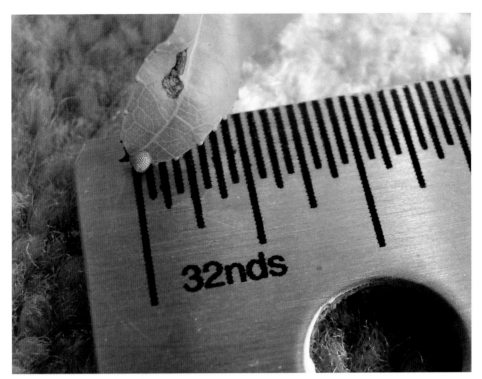

They have 2 - 3 broods each year. The eggs are grayish green, about 1/32 inch, and laid singly on the tip of the host leaf most of the time. It takes 4 - 8 days for the egg to hatch.

When it hatches, the caterpillar is about 3/32 inch.

Young caterpillars eat along the vein of the leaf. They make a ball with silk, leaf bits, and dung, which they hang from the leaf they are eating on. It is believed that this ball may distract predators.

The caterpillar stage is for 12 - 18 days, except for the 3rd instar of the last brood, which overwinters in a hibernaculum. In the last instar, the caterpillar is about 2 inches.

This caterpillar is hanging in J as it prepares to make its chrysalis.

The chrysalis stage is for 8 - 12 days. Before the butterfly emerges the chrysalis becomes transparent.

About 5 minutes after the Viceroy begins to eclose the wings are completely expanded. It takes a few hours for the wings to harden and dry.

Adult Food

They can be found puddling and also feed on aphid honeydew, carrion, decaying fungi, dung, rotting fruit, tree sap, Aster, Black-eyed Susan, Brazilian Verbena, Butterfly Bush, Canada Thistle, Goldenrod, Hyssop, Joe-Pye Weed, Milkweed, Purple Coneflower, Sedum, and Shepherd's Needle.

The Viceroy is feeding on a peach.

Zebra Heliconian

Family - Brushfoots - *Nymphalidae* (nim-FAL-ah-dee)

Flight period: all year southern Florida and Texas, wanders north in warmer months.

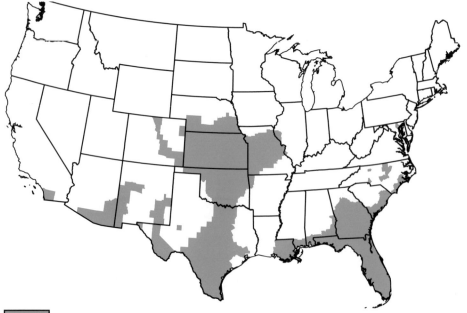

Zebra Heliconian

Zebra Heliconian

Heliconius charithonia (hel-ih-co-nee-us • char-ih-tho-nee-ah)

The wingspan is 2 3/4 - 4 inches.

The dorsal/upperside is dark brown with pale yellow stripes. On the marginal and submarginal area, there is a row of pale yellow spots.

The ventral/underside is similar but lighter. There are red spots near the inner margin.

Host/Larval Food Plants

Passion-vine – *Passiflora* spp.

Passion-vine – *Passiflora* spp.

They have several broods each year. The eggs are orangish yellow. They lay the eggs singly or in groups on the leaves, leaf buds, and tendrils. It takes 3 - 6 days for the eggs to hatch.

When the caterpillar hatches, it is about 3/32 inch.

In the last instar, the caterpillar is about 1 3/4 inches. The caterpillar stage is for 10- 14 days.

The chrysalis stage is for 5 - 12 days.

Adults roost communally every night in the same place.

Adults live up to 7 months. Zebra Heliconians are one of the few butterflies that feed on pollen. It is believed that this is what enables them to live so long.

Adult Food

Some of the flowers they nectar on are: African Daisy, Blanket Flower, Blue Plumbago, Bougainvillea, Butterfly Bush, Firebush, Golden Dewdrop, Jatropha, Lantana, Mexican Sunflower, Mistflower, Passion-vine, Pentas, Porterweed, Red Powder Puff, Sage, Shepherd's Needle, Spanish Needles, Stokes Aster, Thoroughwort, Verbena, and Zinnia.

Bougainvillea – *Bougainvillea* spp.

Common Checkered-Skipper

Family - Skippers - *Hesperiidae* (hes-per-EYE-ah-dee)

Flight period: February - October

Common Checkered-Skipper

Common Checkered-Skipper

Pyrgus communis (peer-guss • kom-mu-nis)

The wingspan is 3/4 - 1 1/4 inches.

The dorsal/upperside of the male is black with numerous small white spots and bluish gray on the base of the wings and thorax. The female is brownish black with fewer white spots.

The ventral/underside is white with tan or olive irregular bands.

Host/Larval Food Plants

Globemallows - *Sphaeralcea* spp.
Hollyhock - *Alcea* spp.
Mallow - *Malva* spp.
Sida - *Sida* spp.
Threelobe False Mallow - *Malvastrum coromandelianum*
Velvetleaf - *Abutilon theophrasti*

Hollyhocks – *Alcea* spp.

Mallow – *Malva* spp.

They have 2 -3 broods each year. The eggs are laid singly on leaf buds, stems, tops or bottoms of leaves. It takes 4 – 8 days for the eggs to hatch.

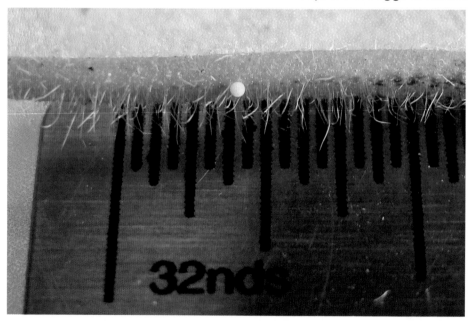

The egg is greenish white and about 1/64 inch.

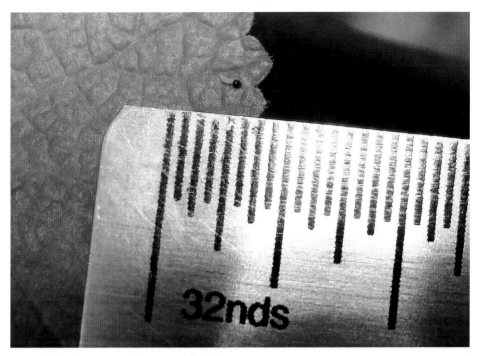

When it hatches, the caterpillar is about 1/16 inch. They live inside of folded leafs which they stitch together with silk.

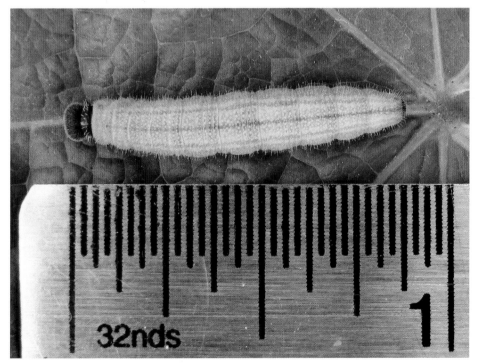

In the last instar, the caterpillar is about 7/8 inch.

Before making its chrysalis the caterpillar's back turns a pinkish color. The caterpillar stage is for 22 - 30 days, except for the last brood, which overwinters in the last instar.

They make their chrysalis within a leaf which they stitch together with silk. The chrysalis stage is for 7 - 14 days.

The chrysalis becomes transparent before the butterfly emerges.

Adult Food

They can be found puddling and also feed on Aster, Beggar's Ticks, Blue Mistflower, Bluets, Brazilian Verbena, Catclaw Mimosa, Dandelion, Dewberry, Fleabane, Frogfruit, Golden Crownbeard, Indian Blanket, Knapweed, Marigold, Milkweed, Monarda, New England Aster, New Jersey Tea, Pearly Everlasting, Red Clover, Shepherd's Needles, Spring Beauty, Thistle, Thoroughwort, and Violets.

Silver-spotted Skipper

Family - Skippers - *Hesperiidae* (hes-per-EYE-ah-dee)

Flight period: May - October, deep south February - December

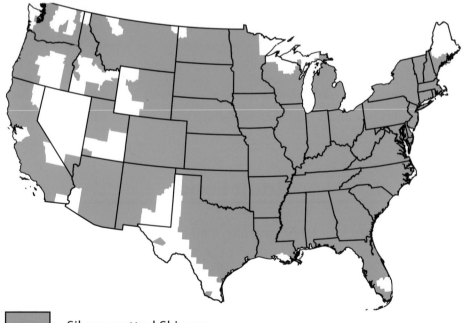

Silver-spotted Skipper

Silver-spotted Skipper

Epargyreus clarus (eh-par-jy-ree-us • clar-us)

The wingspan is 1 3/4 - 2 5/8 inches.

The dorsal/upperside is brown with checked wing fringe. The forewing has gold spots across the median. The hindwing is lobed.

The ventral/underside is similar to the dorsal with a large silver-white patch in the median of the hindwing.

Host/Larval Food Plants

Black Locust - *Robinia pseudoacacia*
Butterfly Pea - *Clitoria mariana*
Deerweed - *Lotus scoparius*
Downy Milkpea - *Galactia volubilis*
Hog-peanut - *Amphicarpaea bracteata*
Honey Locust - *Gleditsia triacanthos*
Hyacinth Bean - *Lablab purpureus*
Tick-trefoil - *Desmodium* spp.
Wisteria - *Wisteria* spp.

She is laying an egg on the Wisteria – *Wisteria* spp.

They have 2 - 4 broods each year. The eggs are laid singly on leaves, and stems of the host plant. They are also laid on things close to it. When that happens, the caterpillar must seek it out.

When first laid the egg is light turquoise green. As the caterpillar develops the egg will form a red ring around it and a red spot on top. Before hatching its head will become visible.

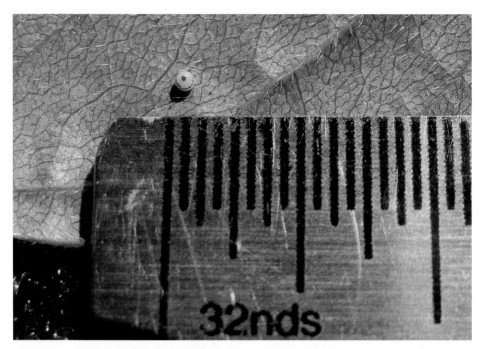

The egg is about 1/32 inch. It takes 4 - 8 days for the egg to hatch.

When it hatches, the caterpillar is about 3/32 inch.

Young caterpillars live in a folded leaf part. Older ones live in silked together leaves. They stay in these leaf shelters when not eating.

In the last instar, the caterpillar is about 1 3/8 inches. The caterpillar stage is for 24 - 30 days.

The chrysalis stage is for 5 - 14 days, except for the last brood, which overwinters.

Adult Food

They can be found puddling and also feed on Alfalfa, Black-eyed Susan, Blazing Star, Butterfly Bush, Buttonbush, Dogbane, Goldenrod, Indigo, Ironweed, Joe-Pye Weed, Mexican Sunflower, Milkweed, Monarda, New Jersey Tea, Perennial Pea, Purple Coneflower, Red Clover, Thistle, Vetch, and Wild Sweet William.

Wild Blue Indigo - *Baptisia australis*

Wild Indigo Duskywing

Family - Skippers - *Hesperiidae* (hes-per-EYE-ah-dee)

Flight period: April - October

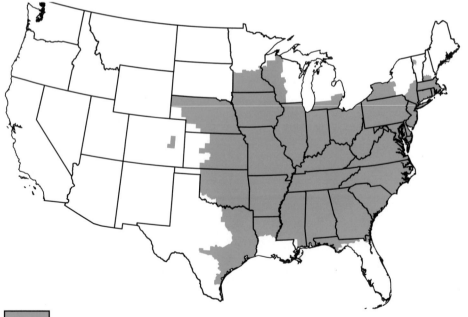

Wild Indigo Duskywing

Wild Indigo Duskywing

Erynnis baptisiae (ee-ry-en-iss • bap-tee-sy-ee)

The wingspan is 3/4 - 1 1/4 inches.

The dorsal/upperside of the male is dark brown with several pale brown spots. The forewing is darker at the base, has glassy white spots near the apex, and a reddish brown patch at the end of the cell. The hindwing has a pale cell-end bar and pale spots. The female is similar but lighter, has a sharper pattern, and larger glassy white spots.

The ventral/underside is dark brown and has two rows of pale marginal spots.

Host/Larval Food Plants

Canadian Milkvetch - *Astragalus canadensis*
Crown Vetch - *Securigera varia*
False Lupine - *Thermopsis villosa*
Indigo - *Baptisia* spp.
Lupine - *Lupinus* spp.

Egg on the Yellow Wild Indigo – *Baptisia tinctoria*

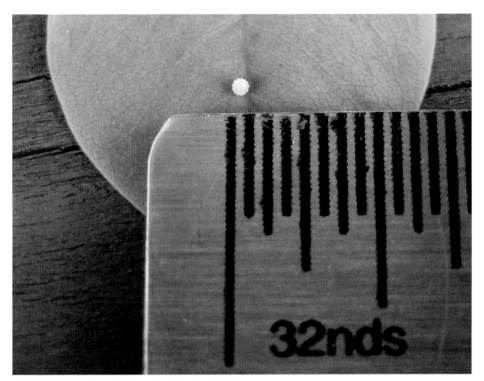

They have 2 broods each year. The egg is creamy white, between 1/64 - 1/32 inch, and laid singly on the host leaf.

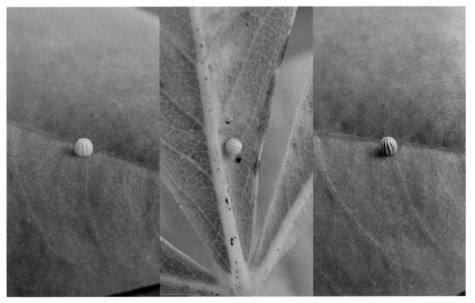

It takes 4 - 6 days for the egg to hatch. As the caterpillar begins to develop the egg turns orange. Shortly before the caterpillar ecloses from the egg, the egg darkens.

When it hatches, the caterpillar is about 1/16 inch.

The caterpillar constructs a silken leaf shelter which it retires in when not eating.

In the last instar, the caterpillar is about 1 3/16 inches. The caterpillar stage of the first brood is for 12 - 24 days. The caterpillars of the second brood overwinter in the last instar.

They make their chrysalis within a silken leaf shelter.

As the chrysalis hardens it turns dark. The chrysalis stage is for 8 - 20 days.

260   Skippers

Adult Food

They can be found puddling and also feed on Aster, Black-Eyed Susan, Blazing Star, Brazilian Verbena, Butterfly Bush, Buttonbush, Clover, Dogbane, Monarda, Purple Coneflower, Sunflower, Wild Geranium, Wild Strawberry, Thistle, and Zinnia.

The Wild Indigo Duskywing is puddling.

Cecropia

Family - Giant Silkworm Moths - *Saturniidae* (sat-uhr-NYE-ah-dee)

Flight period: May - July north, March - May south

Cecropia

Cecropia

Hyalophora cecropia (hy-ah-loaf-oh-rah• see-kroh-pee-ah)

The wingspan is 4 5/16 - 5 7/8 inches.

The dorsal/upperside is dark brown with white hairlike scales creating a frosted appearance. The forewing is red at the base and has a red median line. The hindwing has a red and tan postmedian line. Both wings have a crescent spot that is white to a solid rust red and is tan to brown along the outer margin. The ventral/underside is similar to the dorsal. The body is red with a white collar and white bands on the abdomen.

Host/Larval Food Plants

Alder - *Betulaceae* spp.
Apple - *Malus* spp.
Birch - *Betulaceae* spp.
Box Elder - *Acer negundo*
Cherry - *Prunus* spp.
Dogwood - *Cornus* spp.
Lilac - *Syringa* spp.
Pear - *Pyrus* spp.
Plum - *Prunus* spp.
Sugar Maple - *Acer saccharinum*
Wax Myrtle - *Myrica cerifera*

Common Lilac – *Syringa vulgaris*

They have 1 brood each year. The eggs are light tan to brown. They are laid on both surfaces of the leaf in rows of 2 to 6.

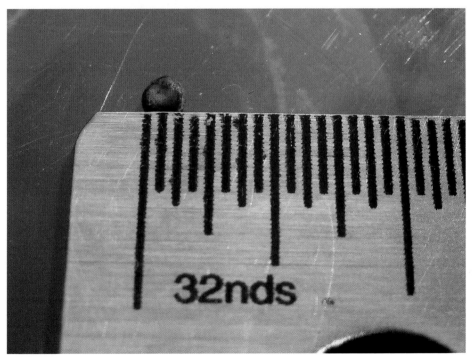

The egg is slightly larger than 1/16 inch and takes 10 - 14 days to hatch.

When it hatches, the caterpillar is about 1/8 inch. The young caterpillars feed in groups. By the 3rd instar they become solitary.

In the last instar, the caterpillar is about 3 15/16 inches. The caterpillar stage is for 37 - 52 days.

The caterpillar is making a cocoon to pupate in. It often spins a cocoon at the base of a bush under thick growth.

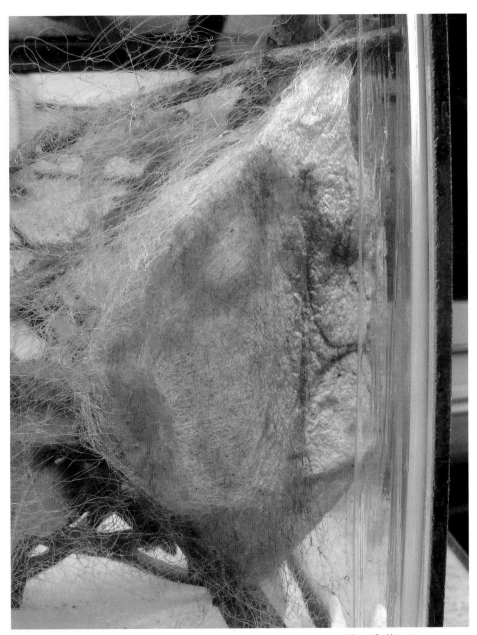

They overwinter in the pupa, within the cocoon. The following year when they eclose from the pupa, it is usually in midmorning.

Adult Food

The adults do not feed because they have no proboscis. For that reason they are short lived.

Hummingbird Clearwing

Family - Sphinx Moths - *Sphingidae* (SFEN-jah-dee)

Flight period: March - October

Hummingbird Clearwing

Hummingbird Clearwing
Hemaris thysbe (hem-ah-ris • thiz-bee)

The wingspan is 1 1/2 - 2 3/16 inches.

The dorsal/upperside of the thorax is olive or golden olive and the abdomen is reddish brown. The forewing cell is either covered or has a bisecting line. Both the forewings and the hindwings have unscaled areas with reddish brown borders.

The ventral/underside is similar to the dorsal, except the thorax is pale yellow. The legs are yellowish or pale colored.

Host/Larval Food Plants

Blueberry - *Vaccinium* spp.
Cranberry - *Vaccinium* spp.
Viburnum - *Viburnum* spp., used most frequently

There have been reports that they also use Honeysuckle - *Lonicera* spp. and Snowberry - *Symphoricarpos* spp., however the Hummingbird Clearwing may have been confused with the Snowberry Clearwing.

Old records show that they use Cherry - *Prunus* spp. and Hawthorn - *Crataegus* - spp., but this needs further investigation.

Arrowwood Viburnum – *Viburnum dentatum*

They have several broods each year. The egg is light green and slightly larger than 1/32 inch. They are laid on the top and bottom of the leaf, singly, and in pairs. It takes 4 - 6 days for the egg to hatch.

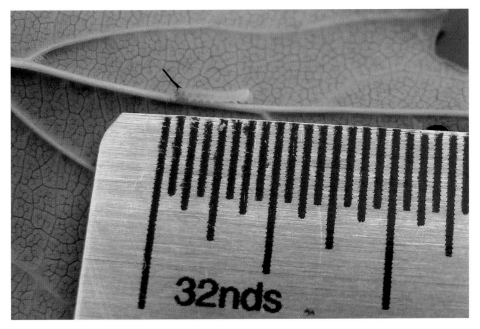

When it hatches, the caterpillar is about 5/32 inch.

The caterpillar stage is for 10 - 14 days. In the last instar, the caterpillar is about 1 15/16 inches. Before making the pupa the caterpillar's back turns purplish.

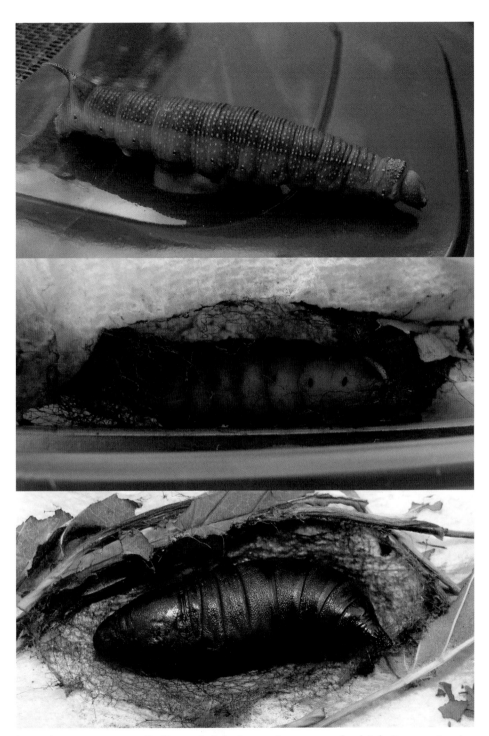

It makes a cocoon of silk and debris on the ground which it pupates in. The pupa stage is for 14 - 20 days, except for the last brood which over-winters.

This is the expansion of the wings after eclosing from the pupa.

Adult Food

The adults are diurnal and can be seen nectaring during the day. Some of the flowers they nectar on are: Blackberry Blossoms, Blazing Star, Brazilian Verbena, Butterfly Bush, Buttonbush, Dogbane, Dogwood Blossoms, English Bluebell, Joe-Pye Weed, Lantana, Lilac, Mexican Sunflower, Milkweed, Million Bells, Mint, Monarda, Petunias, Phlox, Purple Coneflower, Thistle, and Zinnia.

Gypsy Moth

Family - Tussock Moths - *Lymantriidae* (ly-MAHN-tri-ah-dee)

Flight period: July - August

They have been recorded from Nova Scotia as far south as Florida, west as Missouri, and north as Minnesota.

Gypsy Moth
Lymantria dispar (ly-mahn-tri-ah • dis-par)

The wingspan is 1 3/16 - 1 9/16 inches male, 2 3/16 - 2 5/8 inches female.

The dorsal/upperside of the male's forewing is brown with a yellowish overlay and darker brown scalloped lines and spots. His hindwing is yellowish to reddish brown. He has a thin abdomen.

The dorsal/upperside of the female is whitish with dark scalloped lines and spots. She has a large abdomen.

Host/Larval Food Plants

There are over 500 recorded food plants. Oak is preferred, but here are just a few of the others: Alder, Apple, Basswood, Beech, Birch, Box Elder, Hawthorn, Hazelnut, Hickory, Larch, Mountain Ash, Poplar, Rose Bush, Sumac, Willow, and Witch Hazel.

In peak years, they can defoliate large sections of forest. They are also a threat to the nation's conifer forests. These are very destructive.

They were deliberately brought to Boston Massachusetts from Europe in 1869, to raise for silk production. Unfortunately, some escaped.

The only reason that I put information about the Gypsy Moth in this book is to prevent anyone from accidently raising them.

Immature Stages

They have 1 brood each year. The eggs overwinter. The following year the eggs hatch, and the caterpillars are full grown by May and June. In the last instar, they are about 2 1/8 inches.

Their hairs are allergenic, especially if they come in contact with eyes or sensitive skin.

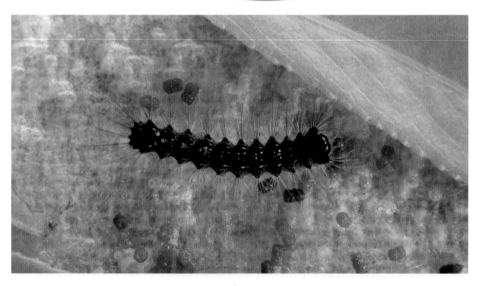

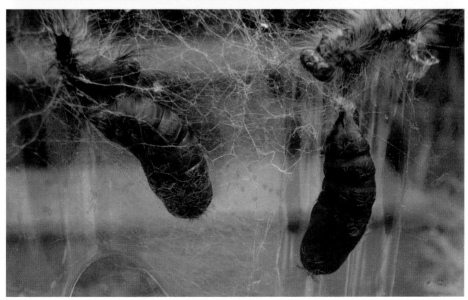

Glossary

Abdomen: The third main body part of the butterfly and moth.

Antenna: Sensory appendage on the butterflies and moths head used for touching and smelling. (plural: antennae)

Aestivate: A type of summer hibernation.

Brood: A generation of young.

Caterpillar: The second stage of the butterflies and moths life cycle, also called larva. (plural: larvae)

Cell: An area on the wing that is encircled by veins.

Chrysalis: A hard case that lacks a protective covering, in which a caterpillar transforms into a butterfly or moth. (plural: chrysalises) This is also called pupa. (plural: pupae)

Claspers: Appendages at the end of the abdomen of males which clasp the female during mating.

Cocoon: A silken covering that protects the pupa as it transforms from a caterpillar to a moth.

Cremaster: A structure that contains small hooks, at the end of the caterpillar's abdomen, which is used to attach the pupa to a silk pad.

Diapause: A state of dormancy, usually in winter, often induced by reduced daylight hours which protects them from long periods of inclement weather.

Diurnal: Active during the day.

Dorsal: Upperside of the butterfly and moth.

Eclose: To emerge from an egg or a pupa.

Epidermis: The outermost layer of cells covering the leaves

Exoskeleton: The hard external covering of the caterpillar, pupa, and adult.

Forewings: The pair of wings that are attached to the thorax closest to the head.

Frass: Caterpillar poop.

Genus: A group of species that have a significant number of similar or the same characteristics. (plural: genera)

Hibernaculum: A silken shelter in which caterpillars hibernate or aestivate.

Hindwings: The pair of wings that are attached to the thorax closest to the abdomen.

Host Plant: A specific species of plants required by the caterpillar for food.

Imago: Adult

Instar: Periods of growth between molting.

Larva: The caterpillar stage of butterflies and moths.

Lepidoptera: The order of insects that includes butterflies and moths.

Lepidopterist: A person who studies butterflies and moths.

Life Cycle: The stages of an organism from the egg stage to its death as an adult.

Meconium: The first excretion of an adult after eclosing from the pupa.

Metamorphosis: The process of changing from egg to adult.

Mexophyll: Most of the tissue between the upper and lower epidermis layers of a leaf.

Molting: The process of shedding the exoskeleton.

Nectar Plants: Food for the butterflies and moths.

Nocturnal: Active during the night.

Ocelli: The simple eyes of caterpillars which can only tell whether it is day or night.

Osmeterium: An orangish forked gland behind the head, which emits a foul scent to repel predators.

Oviposit: To lay eggs.

Ovum: egg

Proboscis: A coiled sucking tube which adults use for feeding.

Prolegs: Fleshy legs, with very small hooks, located on the abdomen.

Puddling: The act of ingesting minerals from damp sand, soil, mulch, and the like.

Pupa: A hard case that lacks a protective covering, in which a caterpillar transforms into a butterfly or moth. (plural: pupae)

Pupate: Changing from a caterpillar to a pupa.

Setae: Bristles, hair like projections.

Spiracles: Holes in the sides of the thorax and abdomen that the caterpillars receive oxygen through.

Spinneret: A silk-producing gland located in the mouthparts of caterpillars.

Spp.: Species

Thorax: The second main body part of the butterfly and moth.

Var.: Variety

Ventral: Underside of the butterfly and moth.

How to Contact the Author

Butterflies In The Garden
Website: http://butterfliesinthegarden.com

This book can be purchased from the website, http://ButterfliesInThe-Garden.com.

Brenda Dziedzic
Email: HappyButterflying@yahoo.com

Useful Websites

Bug Life Cycles
Website: www.buglifecycles.com

Butterflies and Moths of North America
Website: www.butterfliesandmoths.org

Michigan Native Plant Producers Association
Website: http://www.mnppa.org

Monarch Watch
Website: http://monarchwatch.org
Email: monarch@ku.edu
Blog: http://monarchwatch.org/blog
Forums: http://monarchwatch.org/forums
Facebook: http://monarchwatch.org/facebook
Twitter: http://monarchwatch.org/twitter
Amazon: http://monarchwatch.org/amazon
Shop: http://monarchwatch.org/shop
Donate: http://monarchwatch.org/donate

North American Butterfly Association
Website: http://naba.org
4 Delaware Road
Morristown, NJ 07960

References

General:

Bug Life Cycles
Website: www.buglifecycles.com

Butterflies and Moths of North America
Website: www.butterfliesandmoths.org

Covell, Charles V. Jr. 2005. A Field Guide to Moths of Eastern North America. Martinsville, VA: Virginia Museum of Natural History.

Daniels, Jaret C. 2005. Butterflies of Michigan: Field Guide. Cambridge, MN: Adventure Publications, Inc.

Douglas, Matthew M. & Douglas, Jonathan M. 2005. Butterflies of the Great Lakes Region. Ann Arbor, MI: The University of Michigan Press.

Nielsen, Mogens C. 1999. Michigan Butterflies and Skippers. East Lansing, MI: Michigan State University Extension.

Scott, James A. 1986. The Butterflies of North America: A Natural History and Field Guide. Standford CA: Stanford University Press.

Tuskes, Paul M., Tuttle, James P., and Collins, Michael M. 1996. The Wild Silk Moths of North America: A Natural History of the Saturniidae of the United States and Canada. Ithaca NY: Cornell University Press.

Tuttle, James P. 2007. The Hawk Moths of North America: A Natural History Study of the Sphingidae of the United States and Canada. Lawrence, KS: Allen Press.

Wagner, David L. 2005. Caterpillars of Eastern North America. Princeton, NJ: Princeton University Press.

Host/Larval Food Plant Index

Butterfly and Moth Index